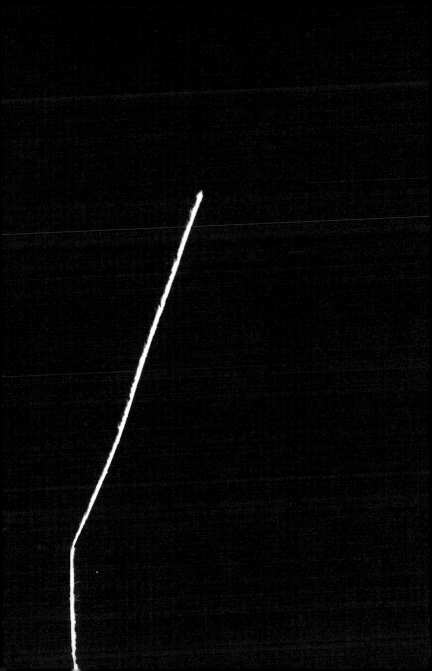

WHEN GOD PRAYS

WHEN GOD PRAYS

SKIP HEITZIG

Visit Tyndale's exciting Web site at www.tyndale.com

When God Prays

Copyright © 2003 by Skip Heitzig. All rights reserved.

Designed by Julie Chen

Edited by Dave Lindstedt

Author photograph taken by Frank Frost Photography. All rights reserved.

Library of Congress Cataloging-in-Publication Data

Heitzig, Skip.
  When God prays / Skip Heitzig.
    p. cm.
Includes bibliographical references.
  ISBN 0-8423-3724-5
  BV210.3.H45 2003
  248.3′2—dc21   2002156724

Printed in the United States of America

08   07   06   05   04   03
8   7   6   5   4   3   2   1

CONTENTS

A PRAYER FROM
GROUND ZERO

The scent of death—it's an unmistakable smell. I remember it from my days in medical training at the San Bernardino County Medical Center. I remember it from standing near a mass grave in the war-torn country of Rwanda, where I served briefly as a relief worker. I experienced it again in Mogadishu, Somalia, when the United States military was involved in a military campaign there and I was asked to help survey a medical clinic for children. I knew it then and I could detect it now as I approached the site in lower Manhattan where the twin towers of the World Trade Center once stood—a place that soon earned the infamous title of "ground zero." This grim pile of rubble and smoking debris bore the stench of burned offices, pulverized concrete, and human decay.

I arrived a few days after the attack as part of the Red Cross relief effort. I had been asked to help launch the Billy Graham Prayer Center in Manhattan, and the Red Cross was training and using all available personnel in the area to support the rescue workers and families of the victims. Our job was to attend to workers' needs at the cleanup site. We carried bottled water to the bone-weary firefighters who were sifting through the rubble in search of any signs of life. Some of us helped on the "bucket brigade"—hauling bucket loads of debris to be carefully inspected for human remains. We also became a "listening ear" for the many critical-incident workers who had never imagined—let alone experienced—a tragedy of such proportions. We gave them a chance to tell their stories and express their thoughts and emotions, and we counseled them about how to deal with the stress they were experiencing—and would be experiencing for some time to come. Some were fresh out of training; others were experienced professionals who had worked the aftermath of other disasters. But a catastrophe of this magnitude was a first for everyone.

Those who had been on the scene since day one swapped stories of what they had seen. Tears flowed freely, along with red-hot anger. Most of the local rescue workers had lost some or numerous coworkers. It seemed everyone knew someone who'd been killed, whether a police officer, firefighter, Port Authority worker, or one of the thousands who had been at work in the towers when they were struck.

As a chaplain on the scene, I was awed by the spiritual opportunities afforded by the somber circumstances. Most everyone wanted to talk and no one refused prayer. When I approached one firefighter and asked if I could pray with him, his face lit up. "Would you, please!" he said. This man needed to talk and he needed encouragement. Amid the smoking rubble, we prayed, unrestrained by our surroundings. After we prayed, he told me his story:

"I was across the city when I saw the first tower get slammed. As soon as it happened, I came down here, and I've been here ever since. I've been putting in twelve- to sixteen-hour days and I haven't been able to sleep much at night." His face grew sullen as he explained, "A lot of my friends are still buried under all this and I guess I feel guilty. And I keep waking up at night with the same images of people falling out of the upper stories." Tears streaked his dirt-crusted cheeks as he said, "I can't shake what I saw that day. I was trained to help people and I couldn't save them!"

❖ ❖ ❖

A SIGN OF HOPE AMONG THE RUINS

At the end of my third day on the cleanup site, I met a chaplain from Texas who summoned me, in his warm southern drawl, to what remained of the U.S. Customs building, part of the Trade Center complex. Walking through the gutted-out entrance to the building we came to the center core of the structure, which had been torn apart by the impact of the collapsed North Tower. Filtered sunlight sifted through the acrid smoke still rising from the sixteen-acre wasteland. It looked like the devastation that only a bomb could cause. Huge metal beams had been shredded as if they were part of a child's Popsicle-stick art project. The Texan pointed down into the wreckage. "There it is! Can you see it? That *cross* standing up, right in the middle of that heap!" Sure enough, there in the midst of a pile of twisted beams and smoldering wreckage stood a metal cross unmistakably perched as if awaiting discovery. We paused for a moment and studied it. Not crafted by human hands, this cross was a by-product of the mass destruction of September 11. As the multistory structure had been violently ripped apart, this signature-of-a-shape was embedded into the debris floor for all to see. Incredibly, in this place of death now stood a stark reminder of another death—one that brought redemption rather than ruin. Just then the tall, beefy firefighter who had first discovered the cross came to where we were standing and told us his amazing story.

"It's been awful down here. All day long my crew and I have been pulling out corpses and body parts. No survivors in here!"

His emotions couldn't be kept at bay any longer. He exhaled and then stopped for a momentary pause, head downward.

Looking up he continued, "I was feeling pretty hopeless after a while. I couldn't take it anymore. I said, 'Dear God, you gotta help me!' Then I turned around and I saw it—this cross was right there in front of me. I couldn't believe it. It was like a sign or somethin'. I want to show as many people as I can so I can get this thing hauled outta here and made into a memorial. This cross is the only thing that gave me hope in this wretched place!"

I felt that I was somehow standing on holy ground and that this brave fireman was its caretaker. To pray seemed like the most appropriate thing to do right then. I asked the small group of men who had gathered there to join me, and no one objected. We joined arms—two FBI agents, a New York City police officer, the fireman, the chaplain, and me—and thanked God for this symbol of hope in the midst of overwhelming destruction. There in that solemn place of mass murder and senseless death we'd been reminded of the One who came to bring eternal life—and we were worshiping him.

Jesus Faces Ground Zero

Jesus himself prayed at his own "ground zero." In the final hours before his brutal death, he uttered a prayer recorded by one of his dearest friends, the apostle John. Before sundown of the following day, he would be arrested, illegally tried, condemned, and executed. His rugged frame would be brutalized like few had ever experienced. Soon he would feel his arms stretched out on a wooden crossbeam while his wrists were driven through with iron spikes, and he would be suspended above the earth until he suffocated.

In the face of this impending torture, Jesus celebrated the customary Passover meal with his disciples. After spending the evening in close fellowship, Jesus and his followers made their way toward the garden of Gethsemane, where Jesus would be betrayed. As they walked, Jesus spoke candidly about many of the issues the disciples would face after his death, resurrection, and ascension. Somewhere between the upper room and the western slope of the Mount of Olives, Jesus turned his thoughts and his eyes heavenward and spoke to his Father.

Given the dire circumstances, what would Jesus say? In this final hour, as he was perched between earth's shame and heaven's glory, what issues would be important enough to cover in prayer? Here at ground zero Jerusalem, what were the priority concerns of the sacrificial Lamb who was about to be slain for the sins of the world? What would the only Son of God choose to ask or tell his Father before committing the ultimate act of humble obedience? Surprisingly, Jesus asks for relatively little concerning himself, but he asks for a lot on behalf of others.

This prayer of Jesus is a showcase for some of the most profound lessons in Christian living:

> How can we talk to God when life is reduced to ashes?
>
> How can we live our lives with the proper ambition of glorifying God?
>
> How can we stay holy while living in an unholy world?
>
> How can we remain spiritually relevant in a spiritually hostile culture?
>
> How can we promote spiritual harmony among fellow Christians?
>
> How can we prepare for heaven while living on earth?

An old Russian proverb says, "He who speaks, sows; who listens, reaps."[1] As we listen carefully to the personal prayer of Jesus, we will reap great and lasting benefits. In a sense, we are able to assume the role of one of the disciples, eavesdropping on the very words spoken by Jesus to his Father. The veil of intimacy between father and son is drawn back and we gaze into the Holy of Holies, into the very heart of God. But as we linger on such holy ground, we'll do more than just listen; we'll learn effective ways to enhance our own communication with God.

THE PRAYER OF JESUS

When Jesus had finished saying all these things, he looked up to heaven and said, "Father, the time has come. Glorify your Son so he can give glory back to you. For you have given him authority over everyone in all the earth. He gives eternal life to each one you have given him. And this is the way to have eternal life—to know you, the only true God, and Jesus Christ, the one you sent to earth. I brought glory to you here on earth by doing everything you told me to do. And now, Father, bring me into the glory we shared before the world began.

"I have told these men about you. They were in the world, but then you gave them to me. Actually, they were always yours, and you gave them to me; and they have kept your word. Now they know that everything I have is a gift from you, for I have passed on to them the words you gave me; and they accepted them and know that I came from you, and they believe you sent me.

"My prayer is not for the world, but for those you have given me, because they belong to you. And all of them, since they are mine, belong to you; and you have given them back to me, so they are my glory! Now I am departing the world; I am leaving them behind and coming to you. Holy Father, keep them and care for them—all those you have given me—so that they will be united just as we are. During my time here, I have kept them safe.† I guarded them so that not one was lost, except the one headed for destruction, as the Scriptures foretold.

† Greek: *I have kept in your name those whom you have given me.*

"And now I am coming to you. I have told them many things while I was with them so they would be filled with my joy. I have given them your word. And the world hates them because they do not belong to the world, just as I do not. I'm not asking you to take them out of the world, but to keep them safe from the evil one. They are not part of this world any more than I am. Make them pure and holy by teaching them your words of truth. As you sent me into the world, I am sending them into the world. And I give myself entirely to you so they also might be entirely yours.

"I am praying not only for these disciples but also for all who will ever believe in me because of their testimony. My prayer for all of them is that they will be one, just as you and I are one, Father—that just as you are in me and I am in you, so they will be in us, and the world will believe you sent me.

"I have given them the glory you gave me, so that they may be one, as we are—I in them and you in me, all being perfected into one. Then the world will know that you sent me and will understand that you love them as much as you love me. Father, I want these whom you've given me to be with me, so they can see my glory. You gave me the glory because you loved me even before the world began!

"O righteous Father, the world doesn't know you, but I do; and these disciples know you sent me. And I have revealed you to them and will keep on revealing you. I will do this so that your love for me may be in them and I in them."

JOHN 17:1-26

Part One

A LOOK UPWARD—

THE FATHER MAGNIFIED

WHY WOULD
GOD PRAY?

WHEN JESUS HAD FINISHED SAYING ALL
THESE THINGS, HE LOOKED UP TO HEAVEN
AND SAID, "FATHER, THE TIME HAS COME.
GLORIFY YOUR SON SO HE CAN GIVE GLORY
BACK TO YOU." JOHN 17:1

❖ ❖ ❖

*C*ountless books have been written about prayer. Some highlight the reverent lives and disciplined prayer habits of ancient monks or bygone saints. Others delve into the prayers of the prophets and others recorded in Scripture. Still others suggest new templates for communicating with God. Several writers have sought to explain the meaning and practice of what is commonly known as "the Lord's Prayer" (Matthew 6:9-13).† But what about the

† The prayer that Jesus gave his followers to emulate would be better named "the

true "Lord's prayer"—the one Jesus prayed while facing his imminent death? This intimate communiqué, captured in John 17, is the longest recorded prayer of Jesus in the Bible. It wouldn't be a stretch to call it the Mount Everest of prayer, because it scales the heights of personal interaction between two members of the Trinity.

What makes this prayer so remarkable and so deserving of both study and emulation? For one thing, Jesus himself prayed it. This intrigues me. Why, of all people, would Jesus Christ, Israel's Messiah and our Savior, need to pray? After all, he's God, right? But no less than nineteen times in the Gospel accounts we're told that Jesus prayed.

Amazing!

On one occasion we're told that Jesus spent all night in prayer (Luke 6:12). Another time he woke up before dawn to pray (Mark 1:35). After the miraculous feeding of several thousand people on the northern shores of Galilee, some who had witnessed the miracle wanted to make Jesus their king right on the spot. He responded by sending everyone away before going off by himself to pray (John 6:14-15; see also Mark 6:46). Evidently Jesus spent a considerable amount of time praying. The question remains: why? Why would God pray? I see three main reasons: to demonstrate our dependence on the Father; to introduce a new relationship between us and the Father; and to establish a new goal for his disciples.

Disciples' Prayer," because it was given in response to the request, "Lord, teach us to pray" (Luke 11:1).

▨ ▨ ▨

TO DEMONSTRATE OUR DEPENDENCE ON THE FATHER

I'm fascinated that the very One who claimed he could forgive people's sins (Matthew 9:6), the very One who insisted he had a timeless nature (John 8:58), the very One who exhibited his omniscience (Matthew 9:4; Luke 11:17) is seen engaging repeatedly in one of the most fundamental exercises of dependence—prayer.

The key to understanding the prayer life of Christ lies in the unique character of Jesus himself. Although he was fully God, the second member of the Trinity, coequal, coeternal, and coexistent with God the Father and the Holy Spirit, he was also fully human. This exceptional blend of natures in the person of Jesus of Nazareth is what theologians call the *theanthropic nature* of the Son of God. (This unusual term derives from the combination of two Greek words: one meaning God—*theos*—and the other meaning man—*anthropos*). Jesus was not only God and not only a man: he was the God-man—fully God and yet fully human.

As God, he was independent of humanity and he often demonstrated that nature as he cured diseases, forgave sins, commanded natural forces to obey him, and took authority over hostile demonic spirits.

As a man, he was dependent on his Father in heaven and he often displayed that dependence through prayer. Likewise, he never acted on his own initiative but did only those things he saw his Father doing (John 5:19). Jesus agreed to empty himself of certain prerogatives of his position as God and humbly accepted the role of a servant (Philippians 2:6-7). In John 17, we catch a small glimpse of the communication between the Son (who was temporarily on earth) and the Father (who is eternally in heaven).

If Jesus, the unique Son of God, perfect in his sinless nature and able to pray for precisely the right things, felt the need to depend on God in heaven, where does that leave us? Are we any less dependent on God than he was? Jesus prayed openly so that we would be encouraged and inspired to rely upon God. The next time you feel reluctant to pray, ask yourself this question: "If Jesus relied on the Father through prayer, what makes me think I don't need to?"

▨ ▨ ▨

TO INTRODUCE A NEW RELATIONSHIP

After walking with Jesus daily for three years, the disciples had become accustomed to having him around in every situation they faced. If a storm came up on the lake, he could calm it (Matthew 8:23-26). If thousands of hungry people needed lunch, he could produce it (Matthew 14:13-21). If a question arose about paying the temple tax, he knew which fish had a coin in its mouth to pay it (Matthew 17:24-27). Whatever the need, whatever the question, whatever the problem, the disciples knew they could look to Jesus for the answer.

All that was about to change, however. Jesus knew that

his earthly life was coming to a close. Although he would be resurrected and would spend a little more time teaching his disciples before his ascension to heaven, eventually he would return to his Father's presence and they would no longer see him. Throughout the celebration of the Passover, Jesus told the disciples repeatedly that he was leaving, trying to prepare them for what was to come (John 13:33-36; 14:2-3, 12, 28-29; 16:5-6, 16). But they could not grasp the magnitude of what he was saying.

After spending most of the evening trying to bolster his disciples and prepare them for the upcoming changes in their relationship with him, Jesus prayed for them. Boy, did they need it! They wouldn't be able to talk things over with him like they used to. Ministry wouldn't be a free lunch for these guys any longer. Now they would need to talk things over with their heavenly Father in prayer (John 16:24-28). When they have an issue, a problem, a concern, or a decision to make, they will need to ask God directly. Jesus assured them that the Father would not only be actively listening but also actively working on their behalf. What better way to get the point across about their future need for prayer than by demonstrating how to pray?

Jesus prayed several things for his disciples. He prayed that they would be *fortified.* "Protect them by the power of your name" (John 17:11, NIV), he said. He wanted the Father to watch over and preserve the still-impressionable disciples. He also prays that they would not be *terrified* by the upcoming attacks from his archenemy, Satan. "I'm not asking you to take them out of the world, but to keep them safe from the evil one" (John 17:15). He knew how hard it was to be a minority voice against the incessant stream of evil in the world. And he prayed that they would be *unified*—that no dissension would fracture their vigor as a group. He asked that "they will be united just as we are" (John 17:11). Having these prayers answered would be vital if these fishermen-turned-disciples were to survive the future.

Today our relationship to God is much like that of the disciples after Jesus ascended into heaven. For one thing, "we live by believing and not by seeing" (2 Corinthians 5:7). Faith, not sight, determines how we relate to God. Because we don't physically see Jesus, ours is a life of believing as we wait for his return. Until then, we need to be in contact with our heavenly Father through prayer. The life-sustaining oxygen of prayer must regularly fill our spiritual lungs so that we can survive in enemy territory.

Jesus prayed not only for the original disciples but also for the disciples he has today. He prayed for you and me! As he looked toward the future, Jesus said, "I am praying not only for these disciples but also for all who will ever believe in me because of their testimony" (John 17:20). Think of it: Long ago, before you even existed, Jesus had you on his mind. You and I came to believe in Jesus Christ because of the testimony of his original followers.

Here's more good news: Not only did Jesus pray for you way back when, he's still praying for you today. That's right! According to Paul, Jesus Christ "is sitting at the place of highest honor next to God, *pleading for us*" (Romans 8:34, emphasis added). The writer of the New Testament book of Hebrews assures us that Jesus "always lives to make intercession" for those who come to him (Hebrews 7:25, NKJV). The death of Christ two thousand years ago was a *finished work* of salvation. But his intercession on our behalf ever since is an *unfinished work* of protecting and preserving us while we're still on earth. How can we lose with that setup?

Several years ago, I was in Asheville, North Carolina, speaking at the Billy Graham Training Center. On the second day of the conference, Franklin Graham invited me to lunch at his parents' home. With a mixture of excitement and intimidation, I sat in the Grahams' living room as Dr. Graham and his lovely wife, Ruth, reminisced about childhood memories, past crusades around the world, and raising children. *This is too good to be true,* I thought. Here, across the room, was the man responsible for so many people around the world coming to know Christ—including me. He has preached the gospel to more people than any other single individual who has ever lived. Eventually, we sat down to eat our meal. Dr. Graham prayed, returning thanks for God's many blessings, and then he prayed for me. He asked God to strengthen me for that evening's session where I was to speak and to give me wisdom, insight, and effectiveness. I immediately thought, *Wow! Billy Graham is praying . . . for me! He's praying for my message. How can I lose? I can't wait to hear what I'm going to say tonight—it's gotta be good now!* I've often mused since that day that if I thought Billy Graham's prayers for me were powerful, how much more the prayers of the only begotten Son of God on my behalf!

✦ ✦ ✦

TO ESTABLISH A NEW GOAL

If we were honest, we'd have to agree that most of our prayers have a simple focus and a simple goal—*us!* Very often we pray simply because we want something. That's nothing to be ashamed of, though, because Jesus did tell us to come to the Father and "ask" (Matthew 7:7-11; John 16:23). Although there are certain qualifications to our asking, we are nevertheless invited to do so. But mature prayer has a much higher goal in mind than merely taking care of our needs and desires. Prayer's highest aim is not to get *our* will done in heaven; rather, it's to get God's will done on earth. This is what makes Jesus' prayer so remarkable. Although he prays for himself in the first few verses, he spends the bulk of his time appealing to God on behalf of his disciples (including us). His priorities during these final earthly moments are centered on others, not on himself. Also, there is an overarching goal that permeates his prayer: bringing glory to his Father. We will discuss what this means in greater depth in the next chapter, but for now suffice it to say that Jesus' single-minded priority was that his life bring glory to his Father's name. He begins the prayer by saying, "Glorify your Son so he can give glory back to you. . . . I brought glory to you here on earth by doing everything you told me to do" (John 17:1, 4).

Some people treat prayer like a fire hose in a public building: For Emergency Use Only. Or whenever life throws them a curve and things don't flow like they think they should, they pull out the old "prayer emergency kit." You know, "When life gets tough, the tough start praying." It's true that we can talk to God whenever we're faced with an emergency—he won't kick us out or ignore us. He loves it when we come and speak to him about our concerns. But we're not to look at prayer as merely for emergency use. It's much more than that. It's for daily use. God delights in a steady flow of communication between earth and heaven.

Jesus demonstrated this free and open communication with God the Father in his own life. There were times that he set aside specifically for prayer and other times when he spontaneously voiced a request or tribute in the course of the day. Sometimes he arose early in the morning to be alone with his Father before the busy affairs of the day could impose their pace: "The next morning Jesus awoke long before daybreak and went out alone into the wilderness to pray" (Mark 1:35). Other times he sought the solitude of prayer after the noise and the bustle of the day had ceased: "One day . . . Jesus went to a mountain to pray, and he prayed to God all night" (Luke 6:12).

But Jesus didn't confine his prayers to a fixed schedule, nor did he use prayer merely as "bookends" to the events of his day. Prayer flowed freely from his lips and heart like a bubbling spring. When he stood amid the devastated mourners at the tomb of his friend Lazarus, "Jesus looked up to heaven and said, 'Father, thank you for hearing me'" (John 11: 41). After seventy of the men he was mentoring returned from a short outreach expedition around the cities of Galilee, they were excitedly telling Jesus about all they had encountered. In the normal course of the conversation, Jesus erupted in praise: "Then Jesus was filled with the joy of the Holy Spirit and said, 'O Father, Lord of heaven and earth, thank you for hiding the truth from those who think themselves so wise and clever, and for revealing it to the childlike. Yes, Father, it pleased you to do it this way'" (Luke 10:21). And when he was attending his final Passover feast in Jerusalem, while predicting his impending death to his disciples and wrestling with the emotion of it, he said aloud, "'Father, bring glory to your name.' Then a voice spoke from heaven, saying, 'I have already brought it glory, and I will do it again'" (John 12:28).

Here's a thought I want you to keep with you as you begin this book: Our true priorities—the things that are really the most important to us—will show themselves in our prayer life. If we are only concerned about ourselves and our personal well-being, it will dominate the agenda when we talk to God. We'll begin treating God like he's a customer service agent or a waiter at a restaurant—as long as our demands are met in a timely fashion, we're satisfied. But Jesus' concern for his Father's glory reveals the proper balance in life and the proper goal of life. Our lives are meant to revolve around God's will, not the other way around.

SEEKING GOD'S GLORY

When Jesus had finished saying all these things, he looked up to heaven and said, "Father, the time has come. Glorify your Son so he can give glory back to you. For you have given him authority over everyone in all the earth. He gives eternal life to each one you have given him. And this is the way to have eternal life—to know you, the only true God, and Jesus Christ, the one you sent to earth. I brought glory to you here on earth by doing everything you told me to do. And now, Father, bring me into the glory we shared before the world began."   John 17:1-5

❖ ❖ ❖

*W*hat one thing defines you as a person? What are you living for? If you had to express your life's objective in a word or two, what would you say? That may not be an easy question for you to answer. You may need the insight of a trusted friend to identify what really makes you tick. But we all have a goal in life—some purpose that drives us forward. For some it's as simple as wanting to be left alone; for others it's as complex as the desire to build an international corporate enterprise. Whatever it is, it's the ambition that places us on a pathway toward the finish line that we've designated as our goal.

Do you remember dreaming about your future when you were a kid? If you're like me, your thoughts took on a magical quality as you projected yourself into the future and imagined whom you would marry, where you would live, and what interesting occupation you would pursue.

Beyond our personal ambitions, there are communal, social goals that we might seek to achieve. We speak of the American Dream—an idiomatic expression that defines our cultural standards as a nation, what Americans as a whole supposedly want from life. Seminar speaker Mona Moon quotes a survey about what people in America desire. She says we want "professional and personal success; happiness; praise; recognition; respect; beauty; health; wealth; influence over other people and events; to conserve time, energy, and money; and to avoid embarrassment and pain."[1]

Oh, is that all?

Yes, these are some lofty and perhaps unrealistic ambitions, but these aspirations, according to the experts, become the motivating seeds from which our goals begin to grow. According to researchers James Patterson and Peter Kim, Mona Moon's cultural observations are correct. Using state-of-the-art research techniques, Patterson and Kim polled Americans to get below the surface of what they regarded as inaccurate survey results to unearth the deeper personal ethics, beliefs, and values of our era. "We asked adults to play this revealing psychological game with us, to dream their dreams: How would they change themselves if they really could? How might they fulfill their potential as humans? And what Americans said: They would be thin and they would be rich. . . . Greed is okay, most Americans are saying, so long as it's not fattening. . . . People across the country showed much less interest in changing their inner selves, including their intelligence or personality, than they did in changing their outward appearances of weight, body, hair, face, and age."[2] Concern for these external measures, say the authors, are the things that drive our entire culture.

What about the *Christian* American Dream? What goals define this segment of our society? Happily, most Christians express ambitions that differ from the findings of the Patterson-Kim survey. "Among born-again Christians," reports the Barna Research Group, "top priorities for their future include a close relationship with God (93 percent), good health (92 percent), living with high integrity (86 percent), having one marriage partner for life (85 percent) and having clear purpose for living (85 percent)."[3]

These results sound like a sharp departure from the cultural norm, don't they? However, as the pastor of a large urban church who interacts with lots of people on a variety of levels, I'm not sure that the reality is quite as promising as these numbers might suggest. The truth is, to go against the flow is tough! Swimming in opposition to the strong currents in our society takes stamina, a solid foundation in scriptural truth, and the prevailing influence of the Holy Spirit. In a culture that says, "It's all about you, man! You must take care of yourself, please yourself, and be your own best friend," it's difficult to keep spiritual goals preeminent.

✦ ✦ ✦

WHERE JESUS FIXED HIS GAZE

The words of Jesus' prayer display his value system of priorities. As we eavesdrop on his communication with God the Father, we understand what he desired for his disciples as well as for himself. We get insight into the driving force of his earthly life. We see his master passion, his personal dream, his central ambition. Simply stated, Jesus lived to glorify his Father!

Jesus begins his prayer with an upward look as he faces the cross—the culmination of his life's work. "Glorify your Son," he petitions, "so he can give glory back to you" (John 17:1). It is noteworthy that Jesus has only a single request for himself. Most of his prayer is focused on the needs of others. It teaches us that praying for ourselves isn't wrong, but praying for others is a broader priority.

Jesus prays that he might receive glory, but don't imagine that this was a self-serving request. He's simply asking to receive back what was his to begin with. "And now, Father, bring me into the glory we shared before the world began" (John 17:5). Furthermore, Jesus is not asking for glory so that he can bask in it after his hard years on earth. Rather his request is attached to his primary goal in life: to bring glory *back* to his Father.

To understand this request we must understand Jesus' journey. The apostle Paul, in his letter to the Philippians, neatly unfolds Jesus' journey from glory to Galilee to the grave:

> Though he was God, he did not demand and cling to his rights as God. He made himself nothing; he took the humble position of a slave and appeared in human form. And in human form he obediently humbled himself even further by dying a criminal's death on a cross. (Philippians 2:6-8)

From eternity past, Jesus possessed the very nature of God and enjoyed all the prerogatives of that position—including the glory of heaven itself and the rich adoration of the angels. Jesus was accustomed to perpetual praise before his journey to earth at the incarnation. But he willingly left the glories of heaven's riches for the glaring poverty of earth.

Born in the squalor of a Bethlehem animal enclosure after a nine-month human gestation, he left the face-to-face fellowship he'd had with the Father for the unusual fellowship of human suffering. Ultimately, he exchanged the praises of heaven's angels for the ridicule of sinful men. All the while he was on the earth, away from the glories of heaven, the glory of his Father was uppermost in his mind. To magnify the Father became his primary focus, as he reveals in John 17:4: "I brought glory to you here on earth by doing everything you told me to do."

We must be careful not to overstate the boundaries of Jesus' self-humiliation. He did not exchange deity for humanity. He didn't empty himself of being God. Divinity was his very nature. He only gave up certain aspects of his position—for example, the brilliant glory of heaven's environment. That's what Paul means when he says that Jesus "made himself nothing." From a heavenly perspective, that's exactly what happened.

Imagine the culture shock! We get a small taste of this whenever we travel from a developed country like the United States or Canada to a third world nation. We're accustomed to air-conditioned rooms, iced drinks, fast food, and flush toilets. We experience a kind of cultural distress whenever we get outside of our comfort zone for a time. Now imagine leaving heaven's splendor and coming to first-century Palestine as a Jewish peasant and then dying the excruciating death of a common criminal! To be subjected to that degree of abject suffering after experiencing the comprehensive glory of heaven would be nothing less than staggering. To go from heaven's hallowed halls to Bethlehem's foul stable, from the throne to a feeding trough, from the crown of glory to the cross of shame, seems inconceivable to us.

But apart from the environmental differences, the real emptying of Christ was part and parcel with his purpose for coming: *His death would buy these rebels back to God!* It wasn't just that he was *around* the sinful habits and actions of people; he came specifically to *take* all of the world's sinfulness onto his own sinless, divine self. All the pornography that would ever be distributed; all the murders and suicides throughout history; all the hatred, violence, divorce, adultery, cheating, stealing, child molesting, and violent terrorism would be shouldered by the sinless Son of God. "God made him who had no sin to be sin for us, so that in him we might become the righteousness of God" (2 Corinthians 5:21, NIV).

In light of all this, we can understand Jesus' request for glory a bit better. He was asking to be given back the preexistent, prehistoric, coequal, coeternal glory that he had once shared with his Father in heaven.

But how would Christ's glory bring glory back to the Father? Simple: His death would not only be *vicarious*—a substitute for the sinful people of planet earth—it would also be *victorious* because Jesus would rise from the grave three days later, conquering death. By completing this redemptive work, Jesus could then offer eternal life to anyone willing to receive him. As Jesus himself says, "[The Son] gives eternal life to each one you have given him. And this is the way to have eternal life—to know you, the only true God, and Jesus Christ, the one you sent to earth" (John 17:2-3). Jesus' death, resurrection, and return to glory completed the work of redemption, allowing anyone who wants eternal life to have it. This is what Paul was referring to when he proclaimed, "He was handed over to die because of our sins, and he was raised from the dead to make us right with God" (Romans 4:25). This prayer, then, is the upward look of heaven's mighty warrior. His eyes fixed heavenward, Jesus had but one master passion in mind— that the Father be glorified!

◈ ◈ ◈

GLORY WITH A GOAL

Let's examine more closely the central goal that occupied Jesus' life and ministry. What exactly is *glory?* The word certainly has a distinctly scriptural and hallowed ring to it, doesn't it? Yet its definition is not easy to pin down. For instance, the glory that Jesus requested for himself was the outward manifestation of heaven's glory, which Jesus refers to as "the glory we shared before the world began" (John 17:5). He seems to be using this term in the traditional Jewish sense—that of the visible glory of face-to-face fellowship that marked the relationship of the Father, Son, and Holy Spirit before the Incarnation. Moses used *glory* in that sense in his own prayer in Exodus 33:18: "Please let me see your glorious presence." The Hebrew word *kavod,* translated as "glory," refers to the profound, glowing, visible expression of God—the same glory that covered Mount Sinai when the Law was given (Exodus 24:16-17). Jesus was asking for that same kind of glory, but rather than asking God to "show me *your* glory," he was saying, "Show me *our* glory once again."

Jesus also used the word *glory* to describe something that he would give to his Father. He prayed to be *glorified* in order that he might "give glory back to you [God]." What does he mean? Is he suggesting that he could somehow give the Father the same outward and visible manifestation of divine presence? Of course not! The Father in heaven never ceased to enjoy that kind of glory. Jesus was using the same word but in a different sense. The Greek word for glory is *doxa,* which in its early usage meant "to seem," "to appear," or "to have an opinion." As the word developed over time it came to mean "a good opinion," or even "to make renowned."[4] Thus the term *to glorify* someone had the idea of displaying the dignity and worth of that person. Jesus' whole life's goal was to reveal the essential character of his Father in a clear and unmistakable way. He came to "show off" the Father to the people around him. He wanted the Father's name to be honored by the way he lived his life and by the way he ended it in sacrifice. The verse might be better understood if translated, "Glorify your Son so he can *magnify* you."

The way Jesus lived stands in sharp contrast to the way people are encouraged to conduct their lives today. Everywhere we look we see billboards and media campaigns telling us to live for ourselves, think about ourselves, and worship ourselves. We are encouraged to "be your own best friend" and "be true to yourself—after all, you're worth it!" The result is a culture obsessed with individual rights, individual needs, individual desires—the kind of culture described by Mona Moon, James Patterson, and Peter Kim. If God is regarded at all, he is viewed as a first-aid kit or fire hose marked "For Emergency Use Only." To many, God isn't the goal; he's the gateway to their goal. Some people seem to believe that if they "praise the Lord" enough, they'll get whatever they want. Glorifying God isn't their objective; their real goal is glorifying *themselves.* God is essentially reduced to the level of a divine bellboy, a cosmic waiter, or heavenly room service. To live for God's glory is not the ambition of the "Me Generation."

Such self-centeredness is a serious problem, especially in affluent nations like ours—and we ignore it or dismiss it at our peril. In order for our lives to function optimally, we must have proper goals. Like a sailor at sea, we must set proper coordinates or else our vessel is doomed to drift aimlessly. Our Creator designed us to function and thrive only as we align ourselves with his purpose for our existence.

What is that purpose?

Simply stated, the purpose of our lives is to please God—or, to put it in terms of Jesus' prayer, our sole purpose is to glorify God. According to the grand anthem of heaven, "You are worthy, O Lord our God, to receive glory and honor and power. For you created everything, *and it is for your pleasure that they exist and were created"* (Revelation 4:11, emphasis added).

Sadly, a different song ascends from our egocentric, pleasure-driven society. Virtually everything is valued according to its ability to bring us personal pleasure—even God himself! In some cases, church is seen as merely a self-help program designed to meet the felt needs of a target audience. Sometimes even our Christian vocabulary betrays our expectations for God to align *his* orbit with ours rather than the other way around. We often say that a person must "accept Jesus Christ." The truth is, it's Jesus who accepts us. Paul framed our salvation by saying, "Having predestined us to adoption as sons by Jesus Christ to Himself, according to the good pleasure of His will, to the praise of the glory of His grace, by which *He has made us accepted in the Beloved*" (Ephesians 1:5-6, NKJV, emphasis added).

Here's the heart of the issue: Our formal theology too often differs from our personal, practical theology. We may state boldly that Jesus Christ is Lord. And we may affirm our belief in song and creed. But our professed belief may not show itself in our *practical theology*. For many of us, it's quite easy to compartmentalize our lives into sections marked "What I *say* I believe" and "What I *really* believe." Such partitioning may be convenient but it's also dangerous.

Juan Carlos Ortiz, a one-time South American pastor, supplies an excellent example of what it means to "keep the main thing the main thing" in the Christian life. He illustrates it with a story about a man seeking to buy a very expensive pearl. The bargaining begins with a simple question:

"I want this pearl. How much is it?"

"Well," the seller says, "it's very expensive!"

"But how much?" the man asks.

"Well, a very large amount."

"Do you think I could buy it?"

"Oh, of course. Everyone can buy it."

"But didn't you say it was very expensive?"

"Yes."

"Well, how much is it?"

"Everything you have," says the seller.

After some serious thought, the buyer makes up his mind. "All right, I'll buy it," he says.

"Well, what do you have?" the seller wants to know. "Let's write it down."

"Well, I have ten thousand dollars in the bank."

"Good—ten thousand dollars. What else?"

"That's all. That's all I have."

"Nothing more?"

"Well, I have a few dollars here in my pocket."

"How much?"

So the buyer begins to dig around. "Well, let's see: thirty, forty, sixty, eighty, a hundred—a hundred twenty dollars."

"That's fine. What else do you have?"

"Well, nothing. That's all."

"Where do you live?" He is still probing.

"In my house. Yes, I have a house."

"The house, too, then." He writes that down.

"You mean I have to live in my camper?"

"You have a camper? That, too. What else?"

"I'll have to sleep in my car!"

"You have a car?"

"Two of them."

"Both become mine. Both cars. What else?"

"Well, you already have my money, my house, my camper, my cars. What more do you want?"

"Are you alone in this world?"

"No, I have a wife and two children. . . ."

"Oh yes, your wife and children, too. What else?"

"I have nothing left! I am left alone now."

Suddenly the seller exclaims, "Oh, I almost forgot! *You* yourself, too! Everything becomes mine—wife, children, house, money, cars—and you, too."

Then he goes on, "Now listen—I will allow you to use all these things for the time being. But don't forget that they are mine, just as you are. And whenever I need any of them, you must give them up, because now I am the owner."[5]

That's what it means to live for the glory of God. It means that everything we are and have belongs to him and we live our lives seeking to magnify God in everything we do. God's glory becomes our core value. Imagine how the church would look—how your own church would look—if we all started living this way. God wants to raise up a "He Generation" in the midst of the "Me Generation."

3

CHANGING OUR
FOCUS

FOR YOU HAVE GIVEN HIM AUTHORITY
OVER EVERYONE IN ALL THE EARTH. HE
GIVES ETERNAL LIFE TO EACH ONE YOU HAVE
GIVEN HIM.   JOHN 17:2

When I visited my optometrist recently, he told me that my
eyes are changing—not for the better but for the worse!
I've always been nearsighted, and I wear corrective lenses
to compensate, but now something else is happening—my
ability to focus on objects close up is also diminishing.

"Oh, that's just great," I said. "The next thing is total
blindness, right?"

"Not at all," he insisted. "It's quite normal for people
your age to experience this." (Is that adding insult to injury,
or what?) He also told me that my contact lens prescription
needed to be adjusted to correspond to my deteriorating

vision. Eventually he'll have to make it so that one eye focuses on things up close while the other one can see objects at a distance. My initial response was a puzzled frown. "But won't that make me dizzy? The last thing I want is to walk around like a drunken sailor in order to see things."

After laughing out loud, he assured me that my brain would compensate for the vision change within a few days. The brain has an amazing capacity to balance visual input and make the necessary adjustments to normalize what it "sees" from the optic nerve.

Likewise, Jesus was able to live in the *temporal* world, without compromising his *eternal* perspective. Unlike the rest of us, who by nature are nearsighted (focused primarily on ourselves), Jesus lived to glorify his Father. His priorities and his focus immediately become apparent when we examine any of his teachings, his miracles, or his encounters with other people.

Part of our growth as Christians is growth in "seeing" differently. We learn to look upward and outward and notice others' needs. We learn to share the gospel (the good news about Jesus Christ) with the rest of the world. Ultimately, our vision should be focused on God himself, and our desire to please and glorify him should increase. After all, if we are really Jesus' followers, we should have goals and priorities that conform to his. But how do we accomplish this? How do we keep a responsible focus on the world around us while maintaining a clear vision of God's eternal purpose? Are there any specific clues in Jesus' prayer that would guide us? I suggest there are two. First, we magnify God by being content with his gifts to us. Second, we magnify him by being obedient to his commands. These two things will help to change our focus and keep our vision of the eternal crystal clear.

◈　◈　◈

BEING CONTENT WITH HIS GIFTS

As Jesus begins his prayer, he mentions two gifts the Father gave him: the gift of authority and the gift of people. The first gift he acknowledges is "authority over everyone in all the earth." That's quite a monumental statement, but it's nonetheless true. Jesus was simply stating the facts. He had been given authority in Creation. He made everything and sustains everything (John 1:1-4; Colossians 1:16). He was given authority over his own life, death, and resurrection. He declares, "No one can take my life from me. I lay down my life voluntarily. For I have the right to lay it down when I want to and also the power to take it again. For my Father has given me this command" (John 10:18). Jesus also has authority over the church. Every saved person belongs to the Lord Jesus in a special way. Jesus affirms this when he says, "I will build my church, and all the powers of hell will not conquer it" (Matthew 16:18). Jesus will have the final authority at the Day of Judgment. Even though life may at times appear to be completely out of control, with evil steamrolling its way through every nook and cranny of our social structure, Jesus holds the reins of judgment, aware of every thought and deed, and will himself render the final verdict. He declares, "Moreover, the Father judges no one, but has entrusted all judgment to the Son" (John 5:22, NIV).

The second gift the Father gave to the Son was the gift of people. Jesus was referring to those who would believe in him—a group the Bible calls the church. The Father decided that the Son should have his own special people. We are the Father's by election and became the Son's by redemption. Just think of it—you are God's gift to Jesus Christ!

As Jesus acknowledged these gifts, there is never a hint that he was disappointed or discontented with what the Father had given him. Jesus understood his position in the Trinity and his role as the atoning sacrifice for sin. He was perfectly at ease with who he was and what he possessed. Therein lies an important principle for us—the principle of contentment. We should say to ourselves, "God has given me everything that I need in order to bring glory to him. I need nothing more or else God would have given it to me." We may not have what others have in terms of talent or resources, but God in his wisdom has given us enough of what we need in order to please him. And God is glorified and honored when we make the same declaration that David uttered: "The Lord is my shepherd; I have everything I need" (Psalm 23:1).

Until recently, I had a large cat—an unusually large cat. She weighed more than twenty-five pounds and had no interest in dieting. As hefty as she was, however, she was never content. Even after three tiger-size meals a day, this complaining feline meowed like a police siren. More than a few of my friends took pity on this creature, saying things like, "Skip, she's crying. I think she's just hungry!" Oh, really? *Hungry?* The way she screamed, you'd have thought I was starving her to death! Her incessant protests made me look pretty bad as an owner. I wonder if God doesn't feel the same way when we fail to be content with his provision. Bleating sheep dishonor the Good Shepherd.

The question isn't, how much more do we need in order to be all that God wants us to be? but, are we using what God has already given to us? Are we maximizing our time? Are we investing our resources in spiritual things? Are we utilizing our natural aptitudes and spiritual gifts to their fullest? God knew exactly what he was doing when he doled out our attributes and established our callings. He wants us to be content with what he has given us and to be faithful to use what he has provided. When we compare ourselves to others and find ourselves wanting, we risk missing out on the very purpose for which God designed us—with our unique combination of gifts, interests, and aptitudes.

There's an old story about a dissatisfied little pocket watch that was tired of not being seen. Oh, how he envied Big Ben, the massive timepiece adorning the British Parliament building in downtown London. Everyone could see old Ben. They set their clocks by him and cued their schedules to his resounding chimes. With his prominent position high above the Thames River, Big Ben was the envy of every other chronometer in the city.

"I wish I could be where Big Ben is!" pined the pocket watch. "That way I could serve many people instead of just one." So, to accommodate his aspirations, the little watch decided to scale the side of the towering Parliament building, pulling himself up by a slender thread. The excitement of the journey left him breathless. The thrill of being up so high was almost more than he could bear. His tiny hands quivered at the prospect of so many people looking up to him. Finally, after years of anonymity, he would be important. But quite the opposite result ensued. Once the tiny pocket watch reached the top of the tower, he appeared so minuscule that he completely disappeared from view. His elevation became his annihilation.

God made each of us uniquely the way we are for his purposes (Ephesians 2:10). We honor God by showing contentment with what he has given us.

◈ ◈ ◈

BEING OBEDIENT TO HIM

Obedience is an intensely practical issue. It is the gauge of our true goals, the litmus test of our values and priorities. Jesus could say to his Father, "I brought glory to you here on earth by doing everything you told me to do" (John 17:4). Obedience always brings glory and joy to God because it demonstrates our trust in him. It shows our reliance on his wisdom and our faith in his choices for us. It proves that we are confident in his plan for our lives, whether we understand it or not. In fact, it's not too much to say that our obedience to God's command is an outward measurement of our desire to glorify him. We don't just glorify God with our *voices* ("Praise the Lord!" "Amen!" "Glory, hallelujah!") but also with our *choices*—obeying what he has told us to do.

At home I have an old-fashioned Euro-style espresso maker. It isn't the fancy kind with the automatic pump that kicks out the perfect brew with the flick of a switch. Rather it's the old hand-pump kind. (We purists prefer this style.) At any rate, a large chrome cylinder holds and pressurizes the water. Connected to this chubby container is a handle that protrudes from the front, enabling the user to hand pump the water through the ground coffee and into the cup. Because the container is solid metal, it's impossible to determine how much water is inside. So a glass tube is connected to the cylinder to serve as a gauge. It corresponds perfectly to the amount of water inside the coffeemaker. By looking at the gauge, one can tell how much water is in the container. When the tube is half full, the boiler is also half full. Likewise, when the glass tube is empty, so is the boiler. The same principle applies to our magnification of God. How can we tell if our lives are bringing him glory? Look at the gauge of our obedience. If it's empty, then our words, our professions of faith—no matter how glorious—are also empty. Our songs of praise and our orthodox theology are not the measure of our spiritual goals; rather, it's our conformity to God's purpose and plan. Remember: We may have our feet on the ground theologically, but we've got to move our feet in order to walk!

◈ ◈ ◈

HOW TO CHANGE YOUR FOCUS

Let's now turn to something even more practical. How can we pray in light of how Jesus prayed? How can we emulate his desire to magnify the Father through contentment and obedience, in our prayer lives and our lives in general? In short, how can our prayer lives reflect a changed focus— off of ourselves and onto God? Let me suggest a simple four-step exercise to help you get started on the pathway to a life that is more pleasing to God: contemplate, evaluate, calculate, activate. Think of it as a continuum that moves from formulating a plan to implementing that plan.

Contemplate

Spend some focused time (start with twenty or thirty minutes, if you can) thinking about the future glories of heaven—the very thing Jesus longed to enjoy again after his incarnation. To spark your imagination, you might want to take a walk in a beautiful place at a quiet time, such as early morning or late evening. Ask God to inspire your thoughts and let the reflection of heaven elevate your perspective. I know it's not easy to imagine a place you've never seen and have perhaps only read about in rather cryptic terms, but give it a try. Why? Because it's your final destination. If you're a follower of Christ, heaven will be your last stop. Given that you'll be spending forever in its glories, try for a while to picture yourself there. To further whet your imaginative appetite, take a contemplative look at Revelation 21, especially verses 1-5.[†] It might throw you at first to have such a glorious place described in terms of negatives—"there was no more sea . . . there shall be no more death, nor sorrow, nor crying. There shall be no more pain" (NKJV)—but I think these details actually help us get a handle on the reality of heaven's blessings. Because heaven is *unlike* anything we've experienced so far on earth, it makes more of an impact to say that "heaven won't be like that."

I'm reminded of the story about the little girl who was taking a long walk in the mountains with her father. There were no street lamps, no traffic lights, and no neon signs. As she looked around at the stars beginning to peek through the blue blanket of the darkening sky, she sighed, "Daddy, if heaven looks this beautiful from the wrong side, imagine what it must be like on the right side!"

As you contemplate the future glories of heaven, ask yourself, "So what? How does knowing what lies in store for me eternally make a difference in my life today?" Jesus used the knowledge he had of the glories of heaven to motivate his obedience to the Father while on earth. Just think: heaven is the future reality for every child of God— it's guaranteed. But what *isn't* guaranteed is what happens between now and that future kingdom. Once this life is over, it's over—no second chances, no rewinding of the tape. Once you're in heaven you'll never be able to share the gospel with another unbeliever; you'll never be able to

† See also Revelation 4, 5, and 22; John 14:1-4; 2 Corinthians 5:1-4; Hebrews 11:10, 14-16. These verses will provide biblical fuel for your imagination.

counsel, pray with, or encourage another Christian brother or sister; you'll never have another opportunity to make a bold stand for Jesus Christ in a hostile world. The *glory* of heaven is guaranteed, but the *glorifying* of God on earth is not. We have to take the next step.

Evaluate

Take an honest inventory of your life and your goals. What are you pursuing? What do you really want out of life? A noteworthy career? A satisfying relationship? Enough money to fund flexibility and mobility? Are you out to prove yourself to someone—maybe your father, mother, boss, or spouse? What's driving you? What are you aiming at? Some of your goals may be good ones, but it's important that you understand exactly what they are. Plato once remarked that "the unexamined life is not worth living."

To help you in this self-examination process, you may want to ask a trusted friend—someone who'll shoot straight with you—for insight and perspective. Ask your friend to describe what he or she considers to be your goals based on observations of your life. (This won't be an easy exercise and it may not be pleasant, but I think you'll find it to be very helpful.) A. W. Tozer once remarked that "self-knowledge is so critically important to us in our pursuit of God and his righteousness that we lie under heavy obligation to do immediately whatever is necessary to remove the disguise and permit our real selves to be known."[1] Sometimes the unbiased perspective of a third party is just what we need to peel away our disguises. Often other people can spot our *real* priorities more clearly than we can ourselves. The goal of this exercise isn't to make you a self-focused individual, just an honest one; it's designed to help you determine whether or not your life's master passion is to glorify God.

Tozer gives a helpful test to aid in this self-discovery. He advises that we take time to consider the following indicators as a guide of what's most important to us:

1. What we want most;
2. What we think about most;
3. How we use our money;
4. What we do with our leisure time;
5. The company we enjoy;
6. Who and what we admire;
7. What we laugh at.[2]

Calculate

Once you've gotten a handle on your true priorities and you understand the balance between the temporal and the eternal, it's time to formulate a simple plan. What will it take for you to change your aim in life? Don't misunderstand. I'm not promoting a formulaic self-help program, nor am I suggesting that meaningful change can occur apart from the work of the Holy Spirit. But planning is an important component of obedience. You've no doubt heard it said, "If you fail to plan, you plan to fail." Jesus asked rhetorically, "For which one of you, when he wants to build a tower, does not first sit down and calculate the cost, to see if he has enough to complete it?" (Luke 14:28, NASB).

Our contemplation and evaluation should lead naturally to calculation—how much will it cost me to change? What things must be different? Are certain friends or acquaintances a roadblock on my journey of glorifying God? Are any of my activities or habits wrong? Do they hinder my pursuit of God's glory? Am I feeding any unhealthy appetites that have become taskmasters? What must I do to overcome these? Where can I get help? (Again, a trusted friend can be of enormous value.)

At this point, your calculation must be joined with determination. Ask God to help you remain committed to positive change. Why live your life regretting the past? Why not, by God's grace and resources, do something about it? Howard Hendricks of Dallas Theological Seminary says, "From research and personal experience I've come to the conclusion that in every church 16 percent of the members will never change. The tragedy is I see young pastors every day leaving the ministry because of that 16 percent. It's as if they're butting their heads against a brick wall. What they should be doing is concentrating on the 84 percent who are ripe for change. That's where the real ministry of the local church takes place."[3] If you've made it to this step of the process, you too are ripe for change. *Don't stop now!*

Activate

Action is always the important last step. Jesus told his own disciples, "Now that you know these things, you will be blessed *if you do them*" (John 13:17, NIV, emphasis added). Once you've figured out what needs to be done, it's time to make the necessary adjustments. If you've discovered hindrances to your discipleship, address them forthrightly. For instance, if relationships have hindered you, you may want to go to those people and tell them what you've been thinking about. Explain that this process of self-evaluation has led you to some new choices. Gently make it clear that you've misplaced your spiritual priorities along the way and replaced them with things that are less important eternally (bowling, excessive exercise, success, etc.). Your friends may not agree with your newfound spiritual goals, but they will probably understand your change of focus if you discuss the issues lovingly and tenderly. In fact, you might even inspire them to reexamine and reprioritize their own lives as well.

Perhaps in the process of evaluating yourself you've discovered you're prone to complaining and nitpicking. Rather than enjoying his gifts and being content with who God has made you, you've muttered that you could do so much more if only God would bless you like he's blessed someone else. If that's the case, then stop, ask God for forgiveness, and ask him to help you realize that his plan for you is the right plan. Tell a close friend or relative about your plan to change in this area and request help. Give him or her permission to bring it to your attention if you start to grumble again.

Once you begin the process of contemplating your goals, evaluating your condition, calculating what it will take to achieve your goals, and activating an obedient heart, it will progressively become second nature to you. Also, when you invite the accountability of others, you'll soon discover that the process is accelerated. As you increasingly ask yourself, "Will this glorify God?" life will take on a new and deeper meaning. You will no longer be content with living any other way. In short, you'll become mature as you live to obey and please God. One author describes Christian maturity as living our lives to magnify God. He explains:

> Christian maturity is being a responsible son or daughter of God. I think that the mature in Christ are people who have stopped being concerned about their own needs and pursuits and have entered into the global vision of their Father so that they may transform a hurting world. The mature go out as his agents in order to accomplish the aims of the Lord's Prayer, "Your Kingdom come. Your will be done on earth as it is in heaven." It's like a son who is being brought into the family business. Instead of racing fast cars and running around with girls, he finally buckles down and says, "Dad, I'm part of it. It's my business too, and I'm going to work hard and undertake the burden of this work." That is real maturity.[4]

❖ ❖ ❖

GOD'S FELLOW WORKERS

The apostle Paul said we are "God's fellow workers" (2 Corinthians 6:1, NIV). Can you picture that—working alongside the Lord to get his work done? Our contribution to the Lord's work may be analogous to a toddler holding his father's hammer and then taking credit for "helping Dad" do a hard day's work, but God nevertheless delights in our cooperation and participation. So how can we "help out" to see Jesus' prayer—specifically this request—answered?

Of course, since uttering this prayer, Jesus has already been glorified, and we know that his atoning work on the cross is a completed act by which he glorified his Father. But I'd like to offer a few suggestions about how we can "weigh in" today in support of this prayer request by our Savior.

Accept Our Salvation

First of all, because Christ's work on earth was to glorify his Father by giving eternal life to those whom the Father had given him (John 17:2-3), we should ask ourselves if we've received God's gift of eternal life. I'm not trying to take sides in the predestination versus freewill debate here. I'm simply saying that because we *do* play a part in being a gift from the Father to the Son, we must cooperate with the process. Part of the reality of salvation is our own choice to receive it. Have you done that yet?

When we respond to the gospel personally and make Jesus *our* Savior, we become part of the group of people that God the Father gave to his Son. If you realize that you haven't yet personalized this salvation, then it's time to do so. Now would be a good time to respond to the spiritual "tug" on your heart that you've been sensing, perhaps for some time. Eternal life is a free gift from God (John 3:16; Ephesians 2:8-9), but a gift must be received. Your acceptance of the gift of salvation is the first step in bringing glory to God.

Engage in Evangelism

Once the gift has been received, the next step is to pass it on—because salvation is really the only "gift that keeps on giving." Spreading the seed of the gospel throughout the world perpetuates the discipleship process started by our Lord. Not all will respond, but some will hear and believe. As they come to know Jesus Christ, God the Father will be further glorified, and God the Son will have more people given to him. These new believers will receive eternal life, and as they in turn engage in evangelism, the entire cycle will be replicated. When we evangelize, we see to it that the prayer of Jesus continues to be answered. Of course, we won't know exactly who is among God's elect until we reach out, plant the seed, and wait for the response. As the great Victorian preacher Charles Spurgeon once remarked:

> Our Savior has bidden us to preach the gospel to every creature. He has not said, "Preach it only to the elect," and though that might seem the most logical thing for us to do, yet since He has not been pleased to stamp the elect in their foreheads or put any distinctive mark upon them, it would be an impossible task for us to perform. When we preach the gospel to every creature, the gospel

makes its own division, and Christ's sheep hear his voice and follow him.[5]

Worship God

Finally, we should worship God and thank him for his tremendous plan of granting eternal life to us by faith. Think of it: Jesus sees you as God's gift to him! The next time you're about to fall over the precipice of self-pity and despair because you think no one cares about you, think about this: It pleased the Father to give you the gift of eternal life and then give you *as a gift* to his Son. Moreover, Jesus has freely accepted you as his own, and he plans to hold on to his gifts! As you consider such lofty truths, your focus can't help but change. When you understand how God the Father and Christ the Son see you, your own perspective on yourself will be forever altered and your motivation for living your life will be properly adjusted.

So thank God the Father, God the Son, and God the Holy Spirit for the glory they have revealed and the glory we are looking forward to in heaven. Let such worship fall freely from your lips when God faithfully reminds you of these things.

Jesus was *propelled* by love for his Father—and we should be too. Jesus was *consumed* with "the family business"—and as adopted sons and daughters, we should be too. Jesus lived to please his Father—and we should be too. After all, we are his disciples. When we live our lives according to God's purpose, life makes sense because we've discovered the secret of glorifying God.

4

PRACTICING THE PRESENCE OF GOD

MY PRAYER IS NOT FOR THE WORLD, BUT
FOR THOSE YOU HAVE GIVEN ME, BECAUSE
THEY BELONG TO YOU. AND ALL OF THEM,
SINCE THEY ARE MINE, BELONG TO YOU; AND
YOU HAVE GIVEN THEM BACK TO ME, SO
THEY ARE MY GLORY! NOW I AM DEPARTING
THE WORLD; I AM LEAVING THEM BEHIND
AND COMING TO YOU. HOLY FATHER, KEEP
THEM AND CARE FOR THEM—ALL THOSE YOU
HAVE GIVEN ME—SO THAT THEY WILL BE
UNITED JUST AS WE ARE. DURING MY TIME
HERE, I HAVE KEPT THEM SAFE. I GUARDED
THEM SO THAT NOT ONE WAS LOST, EXCEPT
THE ONE HEADED FOR DESTRUCTION, AS THE
SCRIPTURES FORETOLD.

And now I am coming to you. I have told them many things while I was with them so they would be filled with my joy. I have given them your word. And the world hates them because they do not belong to the world, just as I do not. I'm not asking you to take them out of the world, but to keep them safe from the evil one. They are not part of this world any more than I am. Make them pure and holy by teaching them your words of truth. As you sent me into the world, I am sending them into the world.   John 17:9-18

❖ ❖ ❖

Tim was a budding fifteen-year-old, growing up in the nurturing shelter of a stable, Christian home. His parents, Jerry and Lorraine, had been converted during the 1960s, when peace, revolution, and drugs were synonymous with a generation's search for a new, experimental way of life. But Jerry and Lorraine had found peace in a relationship with Christ and were determined to raise their son in an environment that would protect him from the sordid mistakes they had made and the "worldly ways" to which they had fallen prey. Their intentions were good, but their plan wasn't flawless.

At church, Tim heard the riveting tales of other converts, some only a few years older than he was, who had left a life full of promiscuity, drug addiction, and cross-country wanderings. Their accounts of dramatic change made an impression on Tim. Some would weep as they told of their former emptiness after a sexual encounter or an LSD high. The applause for these testimonials was always fervent and loud, usually accompanied by affirmations from the congregation like "Praise God!" or "Thank you, Jesus!"

But a problem was brewing inside Tim's mind. He seemed to process these stories differently than most others did. He started to wonder, *What have I been saved from? What dramatic changes have I experienced? All I've ever known is Christianity! How can I be sure that Jesus changes lives when the worst thing I've ever done is cheat on a third grade math test?* These unsettling thoughts simmered deep within his heart for a long time, but no one else knew it.

Then one day Tim just wasn't around anymore. He didn't show up for Bible study. He stopped hanging out with his Christian friends. Soon he stopped coming to church altogether. His parents noticed his abrupt indifference to spiritual matters and questioned him about it. So did some of his friends. "I need to go out and get a testimony," Tim announced. "I've never had one. I've never tasted of *worldly* things enough to appreciate God's salvation." That was almost thirty years ago. I never heard anything more from Tim, the sheltered-turned-wayward teen who would now be in his mid-forties.

What Tim (and many like him) didn't understand is that the greatest testimony one can have is to be *kept* by the power of God. The power of the gospel isn't only demonstrated by major changes from obvious wretchedness to sudden righteousness. One needn't "sin to the fullest" just so he can tell people how bad he once was. When a Christian *remains steadfast* over the years, through many obstacles and trials, it is a significant and powerful testimony; in fact, one could argue that it is the most powerful of testimonies. To stay rooted inwardly in the face of outward opposition demonstrates God's strength to keep us holy in an unholy world. According to Jesus, those who remain steadfast and resolute are his true disciples. And those are the ones that Christ prays will be kept safe from the evil one (John 17:15).

In John 17:9 Jesus makes an unusual statement. He says, "My prayer is not for the world, but for those you have given me." Does that strike you as odd? Why would he say that? Wasn't his very purpose to atone for the world's sins? Didn't he come specifically as an expression of the Father's love for this world (John 3:16)? What does he mean, "My prayer is not for the world"? Why *wouldn't* it be?

The answer is quite simple. Jesus is not negating the purpose of his mission to the world, nor is he disregarding the people of the world for whom he came to die. All he means is that he is not *at this time* praying for the world. His immediate concern, *at that time, in that prayer,* is that his followers would be spiritually fortified in order to withstand the influence of the world that could spiritually weaken them. He's certainly not saying that the world should never be prayed for. On the contrary, we are commanded in Scripture to pray for the people around us: "I urge you, first of all, to pray for all people. As you make your requests, plead for God's mercy upon them, and give thanks. Pray this way for kings and all others who are in authority, so that we can live in peace and quietness, in godliness and dignity. This is good and pleases God our Savior, for he wants everyone to be saved and to understand the truth" (1 Timothy 2:1-4).

❖ ❖ ❖

THE PATTERN OF DISCIPLESHIP

Imagine being within earshot of the Savior as he talks directly to his Father. To hear what Jesus had to say must have been spellbinding. The disciples got a firsthand glimpse into Jesus' inmost thoughts and sentiments about them. As Jesus recounts the disciples' spiritual journey from fishermen to followers, it is the most outstanding and succinct description of discipleship found in all the New Testament.

Jesus prays, "I have told these men about you. They were in the world, but then you gave them to me. Actually, they were always yours, and you gave them to me; and they have kept your word. Now they know that everything I have is a gift from you, for I have passed on to them the words you gave me; and they accepted them and know that I came from you, and they believe you sent me" (John 17:6-8).

In his prayer, Jesus notes a twofold dynamic: revelation and response. He revealed truth *to* the disciples and observed a response *from* them. In short, Jesus establishes a pattern of discipleship: We learn about God and then respond to what we've learned. Paul describes this twofold process in his letter to the church at Rome: "Faith comes from listening to this message of good news—the Good News about Christ" (Romans 10:17).

Let's take a closer look at how it works. The first time we hear the gospel (can you recall your own experience?), we may react adversely, reasoning that we're not bad enough to need a savior or that Christ is only one of many ways back to God. But if we respond to the truth of the gospel, we will soon have our arguments dispelled and will be ready to go further in our quest. To be a true disciple, we must make a decision to respond by faith to the revelation about Christ and about God—which includes recognizing our need to repent from sin.

But it doesn't stop there. In order for spiritual growth to occur, newly born-again Christians must repeat the same pattern over and over, time and again, throughout their entire lives. As truth is revealed about God and about them, they must continue to respond properly to that truth for spiritual growth to occur. The disciples' continued response to the revelation of God's truth kept their lives consistent and obedient. Without this steady and reliable source of revelation, our spiritual compasses would become dysfunctional.

Here's another clock story to illustrate my point: Once

upon a time, in a small European village, there was a clock tower that overlooked the village square. The timepiece was of the most exquisite workmanship and known for its accuracy. Everyone came to rely on the clock's consistent timekeeping, setting their watches by it and relying on its hourly chimes to mark the passage of each day. Then something happened that changed everything—the glass front that encased the clock was broken, exposing the hands and the intricate works to the outside elements. No one knew who had broken the glass, but some suspected that the perpetrator had also meddled with the clock's settings. Soon the villagers began to doubt the accuracy of the old clock. One passerby noticed a difference between the time on his pocket watch and the time showing on the clock tower, so he climbed up and reset the minute hand on the large clock to reflect what he thought was the right time. Later, someone else did the same thing, altering the time by only a few minutes. By and by, other villagers made "corrections" until eventually no one was sure of the exact time. Without the authority that had once been provided by the great clock, everyone set the time according to their own interpretation.

When Jesus prays in John 17:8, "I have passed on to [the disciples] the words you gave me; and they accepted them and know that I came from you, and they believe you sent me," he is declaring to God (for the disciples to hear) that he has faithfully passed along the "correct time" (the way, the truth, and the life) that the disciples can rely upon to calibrate their spiritual clocks (so to speak) as Jesus now sends them into the world (John 17:18).

❖ ❖ ❖

PRAYER: ENJOYING THE PRESENCE OF GOD

What's noteworthy about this part of Jesus' prayer isn't so much what he says as what he doesn't say. He doesn't pray like most of us do. His prayer is not simply a grocery list of requests, complaints, or demands. In fact, when he begins to pray for his disciples, he makes no immediate requests at all. It isn't until several sentences later that he gets to the main appeal for them, which is that they be kept and cared for by God (John 17:11). All that precedes this main request are preliminary statements—factual information about the disciples and their relationship with him. Although Jesus does say, "My prayer is . . . for those you have given me" (John 17:9), he doesn't immediately disclose what his prayer for them is. Could that be a hint about how we ought to pray—indeed, about the very nature of prayer? Could it be that God intends for our prayers to be more of a deepening of relationship than a litany of requests? Think about that. Could it be that Jesus wanted his disciples to understand that when they came into God's presence he wasn't anxious for them to go? They weren't simply to place an order and walk away. God wanted them to linger and just talk to him!

Certainly, God the Father didn't need all the information he received from Jesus. He already knew everything that Jesus told him about the disciples. He knew that Jesus had told his followers about God. He was aware that these men had obeyed his words. He knew they believed that the Father had sent the Son into the world. None of these truths were news to the Father. So why did Jesus take time to mention them? I believe it was for the sake of the disciples—so they would know that prayer isn't a matter of giving God correct *information;* rather it is an opportunity to enjoy *association* with him. Before request comes relationship; and out of fellowship comes fortitude. Jesus wanted the disciples to understand that as they lived out their faith in a hostile world, they could come to the Father to be strengthened and sustained. That's a lesson my young friend Tim apparently never learned. If he had understood how to enjoy the presence of God, he might not have felt the need to walk away from God in search of a dramatic "testimony."

❖ ❖ ❖

A NEW WAY TO PRAY?

Jesus' prayer offers some new horizons for those who would dare to tread the path of discipleship. Three simple principles that give us a new way to view ourselves, God, and others will help to keep us spiritually fortified.

A New Faith: Response Rather Than Religion
For years before the truth finally sunk in, I called myself a Christian. I was enrolled in the church of my parents and their forefathers. I had been baptized, confirmed, and affirmed by the clergy. I participated in all the expected

weekly activities and even some that weren't. In short, I was a religious person. It's a story I've found common to many others like me who responded to what was passed down to them by way of tradition, not necessarily by truth. I'm not saying that all traditions are bad or that traditional churches are wrong. But I am saying that just because someone is a participating church member doesn't necessarily mean he or she is a Christian—a genuine follower of Christ.

According to Jesus, a disciple is one who responds to God's revelation. This is the very epicenter of discipleship. Jesus had revealed to them the truth about God and about himself. But these revealed truths were new to them. They hadn't learned these things through their upbringing or religious training. Nevertheless, they listened and responded by faith and obedience. As the disciples watched Jesus touch the lives of other people with healing and love, as they heard him speak, they learned about God and his plan. They also learned about themselves in light of God's plan. Sending Jesus into the world was God's way of spelling himself out in a language that they could understand. Jesus sometimes used the Old Testament law as a springboard to communicate a new and deeper understanding of God's purpose. He sometimes used analogies from nature or examples from a crisis at hand. He patiently and persistently taught his followers and called for them to respond. And because they were truly his disciples, they did. They came to understand that this new faith was a response to a relationship rather than just another way to be traditionally religious.

At one point, when some wannabe disciples became

disillusioned with Jesus and were parting company with the true disciples, Jesus asked the twelve who were closest to him, "Are you going to leave, too?" Peter, acting as spokesman for the group, replied, "Lord, to whom would we go? You alone have the words that give eternal life. We believe them, and we know you are the Holy One of God" (John 6:67-69).

A follower of Christ is one who responds to the truth. Now would be a good time to examine yourself and make sure you're truly a follower of Christ, not just a bystander. Don't put up a spiritual wall that says, "I know this stuff. You don't have to tell me about spiritual truth. I've grown up in the church. I've heard it all before." Ask yourself if you are setting your spiritual watch by the great clock of God's revelation of himself, or are you trying to reset the clock according to your own imagination and interpretation?

Honesty about your relationship with God will make a huge difference in your prayer life. How can you talk to God if you're not sure who he is? How can you communicate with a God you've made up in your own mind, which is something less than the God revealed in Scripture? A few years ago, *Omni* magazine reported on the prayer lives of Americans. The article pointed out that people from all walks of life are praying in the land of the free and the home of the brave. What caught my eye was the report that even unbelievers pray. According to the article, "The ritual of prayer can even be found in substantial amounts among agnostics and atheists. Fourteen percent of those with no religion pray every day, as do another 60 percent of those with an alternative religious belief. About 38 percent of those who deny a belief in life after death pray daily, along with another 41 percent of those who have serious doubts about life beyond the grave." I must admit, the prospect of agnostics and atheists praying regularly stopped me dead in my tracks. I wondered, "If they don't believe in God, are they praying *to whom it may concern?*" The letter to the Hebrews asserts, "It is impossible to please God without faith. Anyone who wants to come to him must believe that there is a God and that he rewards those who sincerely seek him" (Hebrews 11:6).

Are you responding to the truth about God revealed through Jesus Christ in the Bible? Remember, becoming a follower of Christ is a lifestyle, not a liturgy. It means that we are called to respond to truth with obedience throughout our lives, as we uncover the truth about our marriages, our work relationships, our giving; as we learn about forgiving others, about prayer, and about trust. It is that kind of response that makes our faith a living faith.

A New Focus: Relationship Rather Than Request

Prayer goes much deeper than mere petition (asking God for things). God wants us to depend on him for everything—which definitely includes asking him to meet our needs—and we should never feel guilty for bringing our heartfelt requests to him. But he also wants us to dare to go deeper. He wants us to move to the next level—communion with him. The primary goal of prayer should be to deepen our relationship with God. He wants to do more than simply meet your material needs; his deepest desire is to give you himself. God wants you; the pinnacle of prayer is when we want *him*.

A little girl went to Sunday school and heard a lesson about prayer. When she came home that day she immediately walked up to her room and closed the door. After a while, her mother wondered what was up because it wasn't like her daughter to come home on a weekend and just sit up in her room. Assuming that something must be wrong—perhaps a classmate said something to hurt her daughter's feelings—she mounted the stairs and gently knocked on her daughter's bedroom door.

"Is anything wrong, sweetheart? You've been up here for a while."

"Nothing's wrong, Mom. I've just been praying. I've been sitting up here telling Jesus that I love him and he's been telling me that he loves me and we've just been up here loving each other!"

This girl had a handle on prayer, wouldn't you say? She understood there was a lot more to prayer than simply dialing 1-800-C-L-A-I-M-I-T. To her it was a loving, reciprocal relationship.

Some of God's people act as if prayer were like room service in a nice hotel. They seem to regard God as a heavenly bellhop rather than as a sovereign and holy God. Whenever they have a need or even a whimsical desire, they pick up the prayer phone and expect to get it done. "After all," they reason, "I'm a king's kid—a royal guest in the universe's finest hotel—the kingdom of God." Such an attitude betrays an ignorance of both the nature of God and the nature of prayer. The nature of God is such that he doesn't give us everything we demand any more than a wise parent would give a five-year-old child the keys to the car. The nature of prayer is such that our relationship with God is more important than our requests. Rather than being like room service, prayer is more like sitting down with the innkeeper to enjoy a delightful meal and conversation. The interest is personal rather than functional. Throughout the evening, we learn about the innkeeper, his background, his plans to expand the property, and his personal attention to detail as he reveals his desire for each one of his guests to be fully satisfied at his establishment. We are warmed as he invites us to stay another couple of days for free. We walk away impressed more with the person than with the establishment. One of the reasons that God wants us to come to him with our needs is so that we will "check in" with him more often to enjoy his company.

A wise father whose son was leaving for college figured out an effective way to maintain contact. The boy had everything packed and was visibly excited to be out on his own, away from the constraints of his family. The father had agreed to pay his son's tuition and also to give him a monthly stipend for the next four years so that his son would be able to concentrate fully on his studies. Before the boy left home, however, the father sat him down for a talk.

"Now son, your mom and I are really glad that you're going to school. And, just as I promised, I'll be taking care of your financial needs for the next four years." The father paused for a moment before continuing, "But I won't be sending you a monthly check."

The boy was puzzled. "What? But you said—"

"What I said was," the father interrupted, "I'd be providing for your needs on a *monthly basis.* If you want the money, you'll have to come home at least once a month to get it. I want you to come in person."

This wise father knew that his son might get caught up in his new environment and thus not want to come home very often. In order to preserve his relationship with his son and enjoy his occasional fellowship, he made sure the boy would come around often enough to touch base.

Likewise, God has tied our spiritual support to our regular times of communion with him through prayer. At first, prayer may seem like a free ticket to a game or a handful of candy. But as we mature in our Christian faith, we learn that prayer is much more than a quick recitation of our wish list. We begin to see prayer for what it really is—a source of spiritual strength. Prayer fortifies us and gives us the strength to stand immovable amid the shifting sands of worldly values. A vital prayer life is part of the *staying power* of the Christian faith.

When I was a baby, my primary mode of communication was quite primitive. I bawled! When I was hungry, when I needed my diaper changed, when I was hot, cold, or tired, I cried. No words, no articulate metaphors, just a primal scream was all it took. But as I developed physically, there was a correspondent growth in how I communicated with others. By listening to my parents and older brothers,

I learned enough English to start expressing myself verbally. At first, even this advanced mode of expression wasn't very impressive, just simple sentences like, "I want that" or "I need this." As time went on, I further cultivated my communication skills, as all kids do, and learned to manipulate people. When I didn't get my way, I tried hard to explain how mistreated I felt and how unfair others were being toward me.

Eventually, I outgrew most of that and became an adult. My relationship with my mother today is much different than it used to be. I don't call her on the phone and cry in bloodcurdling shrieks. I've graduated beyond telling her that I want my toys right now, and I've found that manipulation is unnecessary and unhealthy. Now whenever I get the opportunity to be with my mother, the best part is just *being with Mom!* I don't care about what she'll give me; I care about *her*. I love her. I want to enjoy our time together.

In a real sense that's what balanced prayer is like. Instead of being an exercise in self-gratification, it's one of spiritual edification as we spend time *with God*. I enjoy just being in his presence, enjoying the relationship, loving the fellowship. Often I'll go on walks and *just talk* to him. I may not have any specific thing to ask from him at that moment, but I'll let him know what's on my heart, pouring out my feelings, my hopes, and dreams. I tell him I love him and I thank him for his immeasurable kindness to me. I enjoy the intricacy and beauty of his creation in a flower or a sunset, and I tell him! I confess my sins to him and ask his forgiveness and for strength to overcome my weaknesses so I can honor him. I tell him about my day or my week and how I feel about everything in my life. It isn't that the Father needs all this information. He already knows every detail—just as he knew everything that Jesus told him in his prayer. But I am convinced that God wants our fellowship and loves our friendship. Prayer goes far beyond the parameters of asking for things; it ascends into the rich realms of worship, adoration, praise, thanksgiving, and deep communion.

On one occasion when Jesus instructed his disciples to pray, he told them, "When you pray, say: Our Father in heaven" (Luke 11:2, NKJV). That's an invitation to relationship. Jesus didn't tell us to call God "our heavenly dictator," although as Lord he can certainly tell us to do anything he pleases. We weren't instructed to see God as "our heavenly withholder," even though he is sovereign and often says no to our requests. Instead, Jesus wanted us to understand that God is our Father in heaven and that everything is built squarely on that relationship. The apostle Paul later expanded on this teaching when he wrote to the church at Rome, "You should not be like cowering, fearful slaves. You should behave instead like God's very own children, adopted into his family—calling him 'Father, dear Father'" (Romans 8:15). It's time to enjoy that relationship!

A New Family

When Jesus prayed for his disciples, he prayed for the whole group and didn't make individual distinctions. He didn't say, "Father, I pray for everyone—except Peter, who never quite seems to 'get it,' or Thomas, who always doubts everything." No, Jesus' prayer was all-inclusive for those in his apostolic band of followers.

We need to learn that lesson today as the church of Jesus Christ. We have a ministry of intercession for the *whole* church. I don't mean that as spiritual-sounding rhetoric, either. Paul tells us to "pray at all times and on every occasion in the power of the Holy Spirit. Stay alert and be persistent in your prayers *for all Christians everywhere"* (Ephesians 6:18, emphasis added). Eight times in his letters Paul asks people to pray for him (Romans 15:30; 2 Corinthians 1:11; Ephesians 6:19; Philippians 1:19; Colossians 4:3; 1 Thessalonians 5:25; 2 Thessalonians 3:1-2; Philemon 1:22)—nine if you believe he wrote the letter to the Hebrews (Hebrews 13:18).

Praying for other people—especially other Christians—should occupy a large portion of our prayer lives. As we live in and observe our world in all its corruption and with all of its need, there is no shortage of things to pray about. But we must remember to pray *especially* for our Christian family. This principle is expressed in Paul's instruction to the Galatian church as he tells them to be helpful to all people but in particular to the Christian family. He writes, "Whenever we have the opportunity, we should do good to everyone, *especially* to our Christian brothers and sisters" (Galatians 6:10, emphasis added).

We should pray for our fellow Christians for the very same reasons that Jesus prayed for his disciples—because they belong to God. They might not belong to our church or be a part of our denomination, but if they are committed to the essential truths of the historic Christian gospel, they deserve our prayers as disciples of Jesus. Because they are valuable to God they should be valuable to us.

Depending on your perspective, this may take some effort; but try it. As you get to know other Christians in your community and find out what issues they are facing in their churches, become a prayer partner with them. Imagine what might happen if you did! Think of the unity, trust, and love that would blossom if Christians from different denominational backgrounds would begin praying for each other.

A couple of years ago when I drove my son to school in the mornings, I would pass by one of the larger churches in our town. This church is similar in size and range of ministry to the church I pastor, and I knew that some people regarded us as competitors. I was determined not to fall into the rivalry trap, even though, in all honesty, there were times when I had. Because I was driving by their campus every day and I knew that they were facing some leadership issues, I made it a new habit to pray for them daily. At the time, their pastor was leaving and there was considerable uncertainty about the future direction of the church. It would have been easy to look the other way and simply focus on the needs within my own congregation. But instead, I prayed. I prayed that the former pastor would be directed by God to a place where he and his family could be fulfilled and grow. I prayed that God would replace the congregation's shepherd with another man after his own heart, that he would be an expositor who would feed them the Scripture and nourish them in the timeless truths of the Word of God.

Praying for this other congregation was an incredibly freeing experience for me. It helped to crystallize for me my own calling as a pastor. I recognized more clearly than ever before that I was just one of many other pastors in my community, one among countless other servants of God in our state and nation. I started to sense a real oneness with that church and rejoiced when I heard, about a year later, that a man of excellence and integrity was coming to fill the pulpit. He was known and recognized as an excellent Bible teacher and one who was faithful to the gospel. It was both exciting as well as refreshing to watch what took place in my own heart and in the life of this "other" congregation. Instead of feeling a sense of rivalry, I rejoiced that God was blessing his church. Now I make it a regular habit to pray for every church I drive by!

Will you allow yourself to look at other churches as part of the body of Christ? If so, you will discover an interesting mix in this group of believers—a conglomeration of humanity from every race, nation, culture, economic level, and academic level—all in one body. These differences can be stimulating and educational, but they can also be annoying and controversial (if we let them). Unfortunately, we've become more skilled at building walls of dogmatism and establishing our distinctives in order to keep our people in and others out than we have at building bridges so that people from various Christian churches can meet on common ground. Praying for other Christians outside of your own church will ignite a spark of reconciliation and cooperation.

FROM THEOLOGY
TO *KNEE*-OLOGY

The graduating seniors filed into the auditorium in procession—all ninety-three of them. The place was packed with families, friends, teachers, and alumni. With graduation gowns flowing elegantly with each step and mortarboards perched as properly as these teenagers could manage, they appeared more mature than ever. Fathers beamed, though their wide smiles betrayed a sense of relief, and mothers freely brushed away tears, still amazed that their babies had grown up so quickly.

The ceremony went as planned, with one small formality missing: This class would not pray during the commencement. A recent court ruling prohibiting it would now be enforced. Or would it? The principal and overseeing faculty members had instructed the students to stay within the government guidelines prescribed by the ruling. All the speakers gave inspirational and challenging messages, but no one even so much as mentioned anything about divine guidance. No one asked for a blessing on the graduates or their families, either from God or any generic spirit being.

The speeches were nice but seemed routine as well as careful . . . until the final speech. It was the speech that everyone would remember. It was the speech that received a standing ovation. It was the speech that showed the determination of American youth.

As the audience waited politely, the final speaker walked slowly but proudly to the microphone. He stood still and silent for just a moment, and then he delivered his speech—a loud and deliberate sneeze.

Immediately, in perfect unison, the students rose to their feet and shouted, "GOD BLESS YOU!"

The audience exploded into applause, acknowledging the ingenuity of these students who had found a unique way to pray—to invoke God's blessing on their future— with or without the court's approval.

This clever stunt illustrates an important point: No one can really stop us from praying. Where there's a will, there's a way. And when our way conforms to God's will, the results will always be profound. The secret lies in our desire. How much do we desire the results that come from effectively communicating with God, and what are we willing to do to keep the lines of communication open?

I've discovered that whenever I respond appropriately to what God has revealed in his Word, I am fortified in my faith. Obedience is like taking vitamins—the fiber of our Christian faith grows stronger. *Response* implies action, so let's consider how to move from observation mode (simply studying *about* Jesus' prayer in John 17) to activation mode. Let's proceed from the *theology* of the passage to the "*knee*-ology"—actually praying through what we've learned.

▨ ▨ ▨

TAKE AN HONEST LOOK AT YOURSELF

Step one is to honestly ask yourself whether you are a disciple of Jesus Christ. Do you fit the description given by Jesus? In speaking of his disciples, he offers as evidence that these men were "chosen" of God and the fact that they had responded faithfully to what Jesus had revealed. Does "faithful response" to God characterize your life? How have you responded to God's truth? Do you believe it? Do you receive it (personalizing and internalizing it)? Do you obey it? How do you treat the Scriptures?

In Jesus' famous parable about the farmer who went out to sow seed into the soil (Matthew 13:3-9, 18-23), he describes the way different people listen and respond to the truth. Some are extremely excited and emotional about God at first but fail to follow through with their response because of difficulty, shallow commitment, or the distraction of worldly allurements (like my friend Tim at the beginning of chapter 4). It's possible to hear great Bible teaching, read solid Christian literature—including the Scriptures themselves—and yet *not grow spiritually!* The condition of our hearts is of paramount importance and will reveal the authenticity of our Christian discipleship. As

Jesus said, "A good tree can't produce bad fruit, and a bad tree can't produce good fruit" (Matthew 7:18).

It's important that we evaluate our view of the Bible (God's primary way of communicating his truth to us). "It is said that when the famous missionary Dr. David Livingstone started his trek across the continent of Africa, he had seventy-three books in three packs, weighing 180 pounds. After the party had gone three hundred miles, Livingstone was obliged to throw away some of the books because of the fatigue of those carrying his baggage. As he continued on his journey his library grew less and less, until he had but one book left—his Bible."[1] Livingstone knew that if he was going to survive spiritually, he needed to have that one book as his companion.[†]

Based on an honest evaluation of your life, if you discover that you really *haven't* been a true disciple of Jesus Christ, your prayer must start there. Tell God the truth: You haven't been a disciple in the way Jesus described, but you want to. In humble repentance, ask Jesus to become your Lord as well as your Savior.

The next question to ask yourself is this: "Do I apply what I read by putting it into practice?" To put it bluntly, anyone who claims to be Jesus' disciple but doesn't obey what it says in his Word is a hypocrite—a pretender. Wearing a spiritual mask while living a contrary lifestyle isn't a mark of discipleship. It's not how the original disciples lived, with the exception of Judas (and his hypocrisy

† For a more in-depth discussion of how to read and respond to God's Word, see my book *How to Study the Bible and Enjoy It.*

came to the surface in due time). For the early disciples, obedience to Christ wasn't an act. It was their life!

If your self-evaluation turns up hints of hypocrisy, then determine before God and by his strength to change your attitude and your behavior—make it real. Don't hide in the shadows of halfway discipleship; step into the light of truth by becoming a true follower.

Mark Twain, one of the more broadly traveled authors of his time, once made a long and arduous journey to the Holy Land. After he returned, a prominent businessman remarked to Twain that he had a strong desire to make a pilgrimage to the Holy Land before he died. The man said, "I will climb to the top of Mount Sinai and there I will read the Ten Commandments aloud." Twain, who knew the man's character replied, "Why don't you stay home and *keep* them?"

✛ ✛ ✛

DESIRE A CLOSER ASSOCIATION WITH GOD

We've already seen that prayer is not room service, where we make demands of God; and it's not an emergency-room strategy, whereby we come to God only when life really gets out of hand. Although it includes asking for things from God, prayer is more than just a request line. Genuine prayer—like the prayer of Jesus in John 17—is the mature communication of an adult child of God who is content with simply being in God's presence. With maturity comes depth and intimacy. The more you grow spiritually, the

more you'll want to draw closer to God, and the less you'll
be satisfied with anything else.

In his compelling little booklet titled *My Heart—Christ's
Home,* Robert Boyd Munger paints a word picture of the
Christian life, likening it to a house through which Jesus,
the newly arrived guest, goes from room to room. In the library, which represents the mind, Jesus finds all sorts of
worthless reading material and entertainment, which he
proceeds to throw out and replace with his Word. In the
dining room, which speaks of the bodily appetites, he finds
many sinful desires listed on a worldly menu. In the place of
such things as prestige, materialism, and lust, he puts humility, meekness, love, and all the other virtues for which
believers are to hunger and thirst. The quietest room in the
house is the living room, where Jesus has invited the Christian to come every day to spend time with him. After a
while, however, the Christian allows his time with Christ
to be crowded out until simple fellowship with him is virtually absent from his life. Munger, in his uniquely creative
way, writes:

> Under the pressure of many responsibilities, little
> by little, this time began to be shortened. Why,
> I'm not sure. Somehow I assumed I was just too
> busy to give special, regular time to be with
> Christ. This was not a deliberate decision, you
> understand; it just seemed to happen that way.
>
> Eventually, not only was the period shortened,
> but I began to miss days now and then, such as

during mid-terms or finals. Matters of urgency demanding my attention were continually crowding out the quiet times of conversation with Jesus. Often I would miss it two days in a row or more.

One day I recall rushing down the steps in a hurry to be on my way to an important appointment. As I passed the living room, the door was open. Glancing in I saw a fire in the fireplace and Jesus sitting there. Suddenly in dismay, it came to me, "He is my guest. I invited him into my heart! He has come as my Savior and Friend to live with me. Yet here I am neglecting him."

I stopped, turned and hesitantly went in. With downcast glance I said, "Master, I'm sorry. Have you been here every morning?"

"Yes," he said. "I told you I would be here to meet with you."

I was even more ashamed! He had been faithful in spite of my faithlessness. I asked him to forgive me and he did, as he always does when we acknowledge our failures and want to do the right thing.

He said, "The trouble is that you have been thinking of the quiet time, of Bible study and prayer, as a means for your own spiritual growth. This is true, but you have forgotten that this hour means something to me also. Remember, I love you. At a great cost I have redeemed you. I value your fellowship. Just to have you look up into my face warms my heart. Don't neglect this hour if only for my sake. Whether or not you want to be with me, remember I want to be with you. I really love you!"[2]

Honestly, have you ever thought about prayer as being a series of living-room conversations with Jesus? Are you still viewing prayer as boring or something obligatory, sort of a way to pay your spiritual dues? Do you confine prayer to room service or emergency situations? Is your prayer like a child crying for a new toy? Are you trapped in a cycle of tantrum praying, trying to get your agenda accomplished at any cost? Or is there maturity in your communication with God and a sense of personal enjoyment?

Are you ready for a change from the daily routine of giving God a gift list of items you need or things you want done? How about balancing your prayer with the refreshment of adoring praise? In the simplest terms that express your true feelings, tell God how much he means to you. Tell him you're thankful for choosing you to be on his eternal team. Sit for a while in his presence and meditate on his personality. Think of who he is and linger there with unspoken love. Practice "being" in his presence. You may even want to sing a familiar song or write your own very simple hymn of love. You'll be amazed at how spiritually fortified you will be after a session of fellowship like that. It may seem a bit awkward to you at first, but don't be afraid to stretch yourself in this area. Pursue what the psalmist expresses in this passionate refrain, "In Your presence is fullness of joy; At Your right hand are pleasures forevermore" (Psalm 16:11, NKJV).

✦ ✦ ✦

PURSUE BROADER INTERCESSION FOR OTHERS

Cultivate a genuine concern for God's people in your prayer life. That means *all* of God's people—not only in your congregation but also in other churches in your town, state, and nation, and the church around the world. Don't draw your circle too small; learn to embrace in prayer other believers who may differ with you on some incidental issues of faith and practice. In order to do this effectively, you'll probably need to utilize a small notebook, your computer, a PDA, or other means of recording the needs and requests of others.

Begin by thanking God for choosing you and countless others around the world to be in his Church, the body of Christ on earth. Thank him for the other churches in your community that meet the many needs of God's people there. Ask for his direction in serving them. Then look for creative ways that God may be showing you to do this.

When dealing with Christians from other denominations or traditions, you'll need to differentiate between the essentials of the historic Christian faith and the nonessentials that often get in the way of communication and cooperation. Remember this famous axiom, often attributed to Augustine, as your guideline: "In essentials, unity; in nonessentials, liberty; in all things, charity." For example, Jesus clearly taught the importance of baptism for those who come to believe in him. But do we really need to divide over sprinkling versus dunking? Jesus and the writers of the New Testament speak of being filled with the Holy Spirit, but should we refuse to fellowship with another Christian who doesn't entirely agree with our view of how the Spirit fills us and uses us? We must be determined to build bridges rather than walls. Praying for one another—and *with* one another—may be just the ticket to start that process.

Talk to a friend who attends another church and ask for some specific things to pray about concerning his or her congregation. Write down these issues and include them in your regular "living-room conversations" with God. You may even want to write to the pastor of another church and tell him that you're praying for him and that you appreciate his leadership in the community. I'm not suggesting that you neglect to pray for the needs of your own church, but I am suggesting that you broaden your spiritual concern to include praying for other Christians.

We all know the world is full of incredible needs at every level. Many people are consumed with apprehension and fear about the prospects of terrorism, financial loss, warfare, famine, and disease—and the list goes on. There is a great need to pray for such things, but don't overlook what is really needed: The world desperately needs to hear and see the love of God. But how will it happen if not through his people around the globe? It makes sense, then, that a major focus of our prayers should be for God's people around the world, even more so than praying for the world itself.

God's plan has always been to reveal truth to believers and then release them into the world. Jesus spent three years of intensive ministry putting that plan into action—and the church has carried that plan forward through the ages.

Pray for God's people in troubled spots around the earth. Many missions organizations publish guides and journals that provide well-researched information about the worldwide church, including information about each country, its religious makeup, and the particular dangers for believers there. You may never be able to afford the time or money to travel to a foreign mission field, yet through the vehicle of prayer you can transcend borders and reach into places that are inaccessible by any other means. As you "travel" in the realm of the Spirit, you will be fortifying the whole body of Christ around the world and fulfilling the mission that Christ began.

Marilyn Fais wrote to a close friend lamenting that she was having problems sleeping at night. Her friend responded immediately, telling Marilyn that she too had this problem, but that she used her insomnia as an opportunity to pray for loved ones, listing her prayer concerns alphabetically by first names. This suggestion proved extremely helpful for Marilyn. Now as she drifts off, lovingly praying for Adriana, Alan, Amelia, Amy . . . , she says she feels surrounded by loved ones. "I'm not just counting sheep," she says, "I'm counting HIS sheep."[3]

From now on, try this new approach to truth: *I'm going to take what I know and make it what I pray.* Moving from *theology* to *"knee*-ology" is certain to inject vitality into your spiritual walk—perhaps more than anything else has in a long time. Try it and see what happens.

Part Two

A LOOK OUTWARD—
THE BELIEVER FORTIFIED
AND SANCTIFIED

6

LOVE NOT THE WORLD

*W*hat comes to your mind when you see the word *holiness?* If you grew up in a traditional church, you may picture the hushed reverence of a worship service, with organ music, candles, and liturgical ceremonies. If your background is charismatic, you may think of swaying and singing and shouts of praise, along with intense times of fervent prayer. If you come from a non-Christian home, the word *holiness* may be a bit puzzling to you. Author John White gives a classic illustration of what holiness *doesn't* mean in an honest appraisal of his own thought processes. He writes:

> Have you ever gone fishing in a polluted river and hauled out an old shoe, a tea kettle, or a rusty can? I get a similar sort of catch if I cast as bait the word *holiness* into the murky depths of my mind. To my dismay I come up with such associations as:
> Thinness
> Hollow-eyed gauntness

Beards
Sandals
Long robes
Stone cells
No sex
No jokes
Hair shirts
Frequent cold baths
Fasting
Hours of prayer
Wild rocky deserts
Getting up at 4 A.M.
Clean fingernails
Stained glass
Self-humiliation.[1]

White admits that the list is a strange one and is part of the baggage of his past. But he also admits that some of these same words describe how many of us picture Jesus. In our mind's eye we see a bearded saint with long hair and a flowing robe. And even though we don't believe that outward appearance has much to do with what holiness really is, our minds tend to lump these things together. For instance, we'd have a hard time picturing Jesus sporting a mustache, wearing blue jeans, and riding a bicycle or a Harley.[2]

What is holiness, and why should it be important to us? Is holiness essential—and is it even possible in our twenty-first-century world? Is it realistic to pursue holiness in the midst of our culture, or should we seek the nearest monastery in which to live out our days? Can we be holy and still own a TV, an electric guitar, designer clothes, or an espresso maker? Can we be holy and still be relevant? And how does the concept of holiness change the way we talk to God?

Sooner or later, every new Christian realizes that although something wonderful has happened internally, the outside world remains largely unchanged. We may have a wonderful sense of peace deep in our hearts, but wars and violence still rage in many parts of the world. We may have experienced a tremendous life transformation, yet the status quo of vice, anger, selfishness, greed, lust, and terror still dominate the headlines of every newspaper. Becoming a Christian is sort of like being cured of leprosy while still living inside the leper colony. The question we all have to answer is this: How will I respond to the other lepers? Will I integrate myself into the colony and try to help others, or will I isolate myself to avoid being reinfected? Each response reflects a different view of holiness.

❖ ❖ ❖

WHERE IN THE WORLD ARE WE?

"I have told these men about you. *They were in the world,* but then you gave them to me" (John 17:6, emphasis added).

As Jesus prays for his friends, he describes their position in a most interesting way. Mysteriously, almost enigmatically, he frames the battle we all face: "Now I am departing the world; I am leaving them behind and coming to you. Holy Father, keep them and care for them—all those you

have given me—so that they will be united just as we are.
. . . I have given them your word. And the world hates them
because *they do not belong to the world,* just as I do not. . . .
They are not part of this world any more than I am" (John
17:11, 14, 16, emphasis added).

Jesus then makes a request based on the disciples' (and
our) position: "I'm not asking you to take them out of the
world, but to *keep them safe from the evil one*" (John 17:15,
emphasis added). Evidently, isolation is not the key to our
protection. Jesus doesn't ask his Father to hide us or put us
out of reach. Quite the contrary!

What a strange idea this must have been to the disciples—it is to us! Jesus refers to them as *having been* in the
world (implying that they no longer are) and that they've
always belonged to God. What does that mean? How were
these disciples, who clearly were living physical lives in a
material world, no longer a part of it? In what sense could
that be true? It sounds so cryptic!

The Bible draws a clear distinction between what it refers to as "the world," as opposed to the realm of the Christian life. Jesus had already told his disciples that "the world
would love you if you belonged to it, but you don't. I chose
you to come out of the world, and so it hates you"(John
15:19). Moreover, we're commanded in Scripture to "stop
loving this evil world" (1 John 2:15; see also 2 Timothy
4:10). What were Jesus, John, and Paul referring to? There
can only be three possibilities: the physical world of the
earth, the world of humanity, or the world as a *principle,* in
an ethical sense.

The Physical World

When Jesus said he chose us to come out of the world, he was certainly not referring to the *physical world* with its trees, flowers, clouds, and oceans, because that is the very universe God created and placed us in. It is his handiwork. The psalmist declares, "The earth is the Lord's, and everything in it. The world and all its people belong to him. For he laid the earth's foundation on the seas and built it on the ocean depths" (Psalm 24:1-2). When Paul introduced the philosophic skeptics at Athens to "the unknown God," he asserted, "He is the God who made the world and everything in it. . . . He is Lord of heaven and earth" (Acts 17:23-24). Every follower of Jesus is still a part of the physical world and is materially dependent on the earth's biosphere. When the apostle John tells us not to love the world, he doesn't mean that we should despise flowers, trees, meadows, streams, clouds, and sunsets. If anything, our appreciation of these things grows larger because now we know their Maker personally. All of creation points to the glory of God (Psalm 19).

The World of Humanity

Was Jesus referring to the *world of humanity,* the people around us? Does he want us to be detached and aloof from our neighbors, who have spiritual leprosy, so they can't contaminate us with their disease? Of course not! That would contradict everything God said about the people he created. The very heart of God is to love people. We've all heard John 3:16: "For God *so loved the world* that he gave his only Son, so that everyone who believes in him will not perish but have eternal life" (emphasis added). Jesus enumerated as the second greatest commandment that we're to love our neighbor as we love ourselves (Matthew 22:39). So when John later writes, "Stop loving this world," he can't mean that we shouldn't love the ones God loves and came to save. He must be referring to something else. Indeed he is!

The World as an Ethical Principle

The third possible meaning of the phrase *the world* is the one that Jesus intends. By and large, the Bible refers to the world as an ethical system of values. Just like we speak of the "wide world of sports" or the "business world," there is a wide world of morals, standards, ideas, and principles that are opposed to God. It's what used to be called the "spirit of the age," meaning the attitudes and standards that the people of the world hold dear. The *world* in this sense is the system of ideas, activities, and people ruled by the ethics of Satan, who is called "the god of this evil world" (2 Corinthians 4:4). So although we are to love the universe God made and its people, whom God loves, we must never love the system, which is replete with philosophies and practices that stand in direct conflict with God himself. To do so would constitute a conflict of interest—a conflict of love. When John gave the command not to love the world, he explained why: "Stop loving this evil world and all that it offers you, for when you love the world, you show that you do not have the love of the Father in you.

For the world offers only the lust for physical pleasure, the lust for everything we see, and pride in our possessions. These are not from the Father. They are from this evil world. And this world is fading away, along with everything it craves. But if you do the will of God, you will live forever" (1 John 2:15-17). So for Jesus to pray for his disciples, who were no longer of this world, to be kept from Satan's worldly grasp, he was praying that their love for God would remain supreme. Love is the power behind every relationship, and love for God must be the driving force of every true disciple. Our relationship with God must become the pivotal relationship against which all other relationships are measured.

Our Precarious Position

As disciples of Christ, we are in a precarious position. Like an astronaut in outer space or a scuba diver hundreds of feet beneath the ocean's surface, we're living outside our natural element. It's possible to survive here, given special provision for our protection, but this world is not our home (John 17:14, 16; Philippians 3:20). What makes our position precarious is that the world is filled with the allurements of greed, sensual images, and the powerful attraction of selfish living. It's a system that can be downright intoxicating to anyone living here. But if we align ourselves with the worldly system, we align ourselves with the enemies of God. Furthermore, the worldly system doesn't tolerate people who are different! To borrow from an earlier analogy, the lepers don't take kindly to someone "whole" walking around in their midst. That's why we're tempted to flee. But don't. We can't! We're needed here!

If the world around us is ever going to hear the truth and see its importance, it must be through us. However, it won't be easy. To walk the straight and narrow of Christian ethics while living in this world is like walking a tightrope over a cage of hungry lions. It can be done, but each step must be chosen carefully. Consider it an occupational hazard of following Christ. As long as we float with the current of the world's indulgent, promiscuous, agnostic, and generically spiritual ways, the world won't tamper with us. But the moment we stand out by going against the flow of such values, we become targets.

How did Jesus expect his disciples to survive? How will we? Surrounded by worldly people who follow an entirely different drumbeat, how can we carry on in the opposite, heavenward direction? In a word, *holiness,* which is the focus of the next chapter. Just as there has been a lot of misunderstanding about what *holiness* means, there is even more misunderstanding about how to practice holiness in everyday life. In every age, there have been Christians who have withdrawn into isolation, wanting little if any contact with the non-Christian world. Europe is littered with old convents and monasteries, the remains of a time when seclusion was seen as the path to holiness. The temptation to follow in the footsteps of the ascetics is still felt in our present age. In a sense, many Christians have withdrawn into tightly knit circles of Christian fellowship that meet their social and entertainment needs. When this happens, they betray their confusion between separation from sin and isolation from sinners.

We must recast—if not redefine altogether—our understanding of holiness, how it should look from day to day, and how it looks on us. Rather than being sidetracked by past experience, we must set a new course based on scriptural principles. The challenge is to live a lifestyle that is different enough from the world's system that we are not tainted by its values, while at the same time remaining relevant and attractive to unbelievers so that they will want to forsake their "leprosy" of sin and come to Christ to be healed.

7

HOLINESS IN AN UNHOLY WORLD

Now I am departing the world; I am leaving them behind and coming to you. Holy Father, keep them and care for them—all those you have given me—so that they will be united just as we are. During my time here, I have kept them safe. I guarded them so that not one was lost, except the one headed for destruction, as the Scriptures foretold.

And now I am coming to you. I have told them many things while I was with them so they would be filled with my joy. I have given them your word. And the world hates them because they do

not belong to the world, just as I do
not. I'm not asking you to take them
out of the world, but to keep them
safe from the evil one. They are not
part of this world any more than I am.
Make them pure and holy by teaching
them your words of truth. As you sent
me into the world, I am sending them
into the world. And I give myself
entirely to you so they also might be
entirely yours.   John 17:11-19

✦ ✦ ✦

Not long ago, at our church's midweek Bible study, I opened with prayer as I typically do. On this particular evening, our nation was facing a crisis that had headlined all the news reports. The Beltway Sniper, who had already killed several innocent people in the Washington, D.C., area, had struck again, creating pandemonium in the Northeast and outrage across the country. Because I knew that everyone was aware of the situation and apprehensive about it, I prayed that the sniper would quickly be captured and that the people of Maryland and Virginia would be kept safe.

The next day I received a delightful e-mail from a grateful parent. She was happy not only that we had prayed for the situation, but also for the impression it had made on her son. She wrote:

> On the way home from church, I told my ten-year-old son about your prayer and told him we needed to remember to pray also. The next morning, after we heard that the sniper had been caught, he had to call his dad and tell him, "Dad, Skip prayed that the sniper would be caught and God answered his prayer! Cool, huh?"

I'm not claiming single-handed credit for the sniper being caught, of course, but there is a young boy in Albuquerque, New Mexico, who is thrilled at the possibility that his prayer can make a difference. I applaud his parents for not sheltering him from the reality of sin in the world; they took a proactive step in not only informing him of the danger but also transforming him into a responsive Christian believer who can leave a mark on his culture.

A closer examination of Jesus' prayer reveals a strategy for remaining holy in an unholy world. Jesus prays for four specific things for his disciples:

- ✛ That they be kept and cared for by God in the midst of the world—John 17:11
- ✛ That they be protected from evil—John 17:15
- ✛ That they be prepared to face the difficulties of the world by being consecrated by God's truth—John 17:15, 17

✛ That instead of living sheltered lives,
they be sent out into the world as his
representatives, commissioned for divine
service—John 17:18

I'm calling these four phases preservation, protection, preparation, and permeation.

✤ ✤ ✤

PRESERVATION

Jesus was not an escapist. He didn't advocate a monastic lifestyle. He didn't give his disciples a plan for hiding in isolation after storing up food, weapons, and antigovernment literature in remote caves. His request to God for them was simple: "I'm not asking you to take them out of the world, but to keep them safe from the evil one."

This world's system is not static; it is dynamic, active, and ever changing. Satan, the ruler of the earth (1 John 5:19), uses the world's system against Christians to displace their love for God and replace it with love for the world.[1] The world's approach goes something like this: "Hey, you're surrounded on every side; you might as well just go along with the rest of us instead of trying to act like some holier-than-thou puritanical prude!" But we're warned against this. James wrote to the early Christians, "You adulterers! Don't you realize that friendship with this world makes you an enemy of God? I say it again, that if your aim is to enjoy this world, you can't be a friend of God" (James 4:4). Flirting with the world is a dangerous romance that can lead us to compromise our love for God.

However, in our pursuit to find pleasure in the things of the world, the opposite will happen. Happiness will elude us. Since we're now creatures of eternity (Ecclesiastes 3:11), nothing in this worldly system will satisfy us. The pursuit may be alluring, but it's really a trap. The most miserable Christians I know are worldly ones. They are like fish trapped in a net—still alive but bound up, immobilized, and unproductive—and headed for destruction if they don't break free.

When Napoleon and his men marched endlessly through the burning Egyptian desert during his ill-fated attempt to conquer that ancient land, the soldiers were thirsty for water. As they trudged onward, someone shouted from their ranks, "Water! Water! Water!" Lifting their eyes to the horizon, the men saw what seemed to be a lake—an oasis in the middle of the desert. Its waters shimmered and sparkled in the desert sun, inviting them to come and be refreshed. However, as the soldiers ran toward them, the waters receded. Their second discovery was the correct one—it wasn't a lake at all but a deceptive mirage of the desert. The world's allurements never quite satisfy; their illusive images are only mirages.

Disciples of Jesus are called to be a part of a counterculture of sorts—to live *in* but not be *of* the world. We're surrounded by the world's system, but Jesus prayed that we won't be swallowed up by it. Paul tells us in Romans that staying holy in an unholy world requires a change in our mind-set: "Don't copy the behavior and customs of this world, but let God transform you into a new person by changing the way you think" (Romans 12:2). Christians aren't to be copycats, thinking and acting like everyone else. We must be willing to stand alone, if necessary, against the strong pull of the world that seeks to make us into carbon copies. We would do well to learn from the example of Christian, the protagonist of John Bunyan's *Pilgrim's Progress,* who plugged his ears with his fingers and cried, "Life! Life! Eternal Life!" when his family and neighbors called him to return to his hometown, the City of Destruction.

At times in church history, the pull of the world seemed so strong that some Christians found ways to isolate themselves. Some retreated to monasteries, but others found more exotic ways to avoid the contamination of the world. In the fifth century, a man named Simeon Stylites lived for thirty-six years atop a fifty-foot-tall pillar, spending his time in contemplation and prayer. When a Frenchman by the name of Anatole heard about Simeon's exploits, he too determined to go the way of isolated denial. But the weather and living conditions being what they were in France, Anatole decided to improvise. Rather than stake out his own pillar, he donned a simple garment and sat on a chair atop his kitchen table. All was well until his family returned home. They thought he was nuts and told him so. In fact, they succeeded in making life so miserable for Anatole that he decided to quit his vigil. He said, "I soon perceived that it is a very difficult thing to be a saint while living with your own family! I see why Simeon and Jerome went into the desert."[2]

Isolation was never Jesus' plan, nor was it his prayer for his disciples. We don't need saints on top of pillars or locked away from the hum and buzz of life. We need saints in the midst of everyday life—in factories, offices, studios, and shopping malls. Uptown, downtown, and across town in every city. We need saints right where you are now! Jesus insisted that we live out our Christianity *among* people, not away from them. That was part of his commission to the disciples: "I am sending you out as sheep among wolves" (Matthew 10:16).

"What?" you may ask. "What kind of a spiritual leader would send his followers into such a hostile hot spot? Does he want his sheep to be devoured by the dastardly and dangerous wolves of the world?" No! What he really wants to happen is for some of those wolves to be converted to sheep. They may appear hostile, but they can be reached if we will go out to them. They can't be reached if we don't.

❖ ❖ ❖

PROTECTION

What did Jesus pray that his disciples be kept from? It wasn't so much the world as it was the executive director of the worldly system—Satan. "I'm not asking you to take them out of the world, but to keep them safe from the evil one" (John 17:15). Because Satan is the one operating behind the curtains, pulling the stage strings of this worldly system, he is the real threat to us. Through enticements and temptations he will use every device to prey upon our human nature and pry our hearts away from God. To resist him effectively, we must understand our role in the battle. John White reminds us:

> His supreme object is to hurt Christ. You personally are of no interest to him. It is only as you relate to Christ that you assume significance in his eyes. Before you became a Christian, he was mainly interested in blinding you to the truth of Christ, or perhaps in seducing you further into his terrain. But this was not because of your personal importance. He only used you to get back at God. Similarly, now that you are a Christian his interest in you has nothing to do with you as an individual so much as with your potential for Christ's cause. Do not flatter yourself. To God you are very important. But to Satan you are nothing more than a potentially useful microbe.[3]

Of course, Jesus' prayer for preservation of the disciples wasn't solely because he was interested in "the cause." He loved his disciples very much. Yes, he needed them to spread the message of his kingdom, but he also did not want them to lose their joy or be sucked back into the world's system (John 17:12-16). Both the message and the messengers were important to Jesus.

❖ ❖ ❖

PREPARATION

The third thing Jesus prayed for his disciples was that God would "make them pure and holy by teaching them [his] words of truth" (John 17:17). Some translations of the Bible render "make them pure and holy" as "sanctify them." If ever there was a churchy-sounding word, *sanctify* is it. Sanctification refers to the process of being set apart or dedicated to God. The Greek word used here—*hagiadzo*—includes in its meaning such ideas as dedication, consecration, devotion, allegiance, or setting apart for a special purpose. I think Eugene Peterson's fresh translation, called *The Message,* makes the meaning crystal clear: "Make them holy—consecrated—with the truth; Your word is consecrating truth."[4] To be holy means to be dedicated completely to God, even while surrounded by a godless world.

In his simple request, Jesus shows us how disciples can be prepared to face the hostilities of an unsympathetic world system. It's not by becoming like the system itself, but by being different. It's not by trying to copy a worldly lifestyle, but by confronting the ways of the world with a Christlike lifestyle. And the means of achieving spiritual strength is by an ongoing relationship to God's truth.

Here's the secret to success: God's workers, who are full of God's Word, do God's work in the world. This is the road to spiritual strength, the pathway to spiritual power. The only way to stay pure and not fold under the pressure of the surrounding world is by being conversant in and subject to God's written revelation. Only by immersing ourselves in God's Word can we survive exposure to the values and allurements of the world—day and night—without being squeezed into its twisted mold.

Reading the Bible is not an optional exercise. It is essential for our survival. Why? Because the world's system will use every means available to put godless values in our minds, deceive us, and bring us down. The only way to avoid being completely duped by such a steady stream of propaganda from the enemy is to be immersed in truth. We must read it, understand it, apply it, and then *do* what it says. That's how we engage in the process that Jesus prayed for. To stem the strong current of the river of deception, our lives must be firmly tied to the moorings of God's truth.

God's Word tells us the truth about the world in which we live. It deals honestly with who we are and what we need to do. The Bible reveals our problems as well as the solution. God's truth confronts us and sometimes rebukes us. It also comforts and consoles us. God's consecrating truth is what prepares us to stay afloat in the murky waters of a world that has lost sight of God. Without God's consecrating truth in our hearts, we are doomed to despair and conformity to the "leper colonies" of this world. Dwight L. Moody, the nineteenth-century American evangelist, said of the Bible, "Sin will keep you from this book. This book will keep you from sin."[5] He may well have been thinking about David's words in Psalm 119:11: "I have hidden your word in my heart, that I might not sin against you." Just as an antibiotic offsets the undermining work of an infection, so God's truth overcomes the malicious effects of worldly deception.

❖ ❖ ❖

PERMEATION

There is yet another purpose for Jesus' first two requests. There is more to our being "kept" than just our survival. The whole purpose of preparing ourselves with God's consecrating truth is so we'll be equipped to go into the world and rescue souls. God still cares about the world he created. He still loves the people who hate him. Jesus said, "As you sent me into the world, I am sending them into the world" (John 17:18). His rescue and recovery operation includes us.

During the reign of Oliver Cromwell, the British government ran out of silver to make coins. Cromwell responded to the need by sending his men across the nation to see if they could uncover more of the precious metal. They returned shortly without much to speak of, reporting that the only silver they could find was in the statues of the saints that were on display in sundry cathedrals around England. "Good!" replied Cromwell. "Then we will melt down the saints and put them back into circulation!"[6]

Jesus doesn't want his disciples to be "statues on display" in church groups, touting their spiritual prowess to one another. We're not to become religious museum pieces. Rather, we're to be a base of operations that equips God's people so that they may be deployed into the world.

We need to spend time in the Word, soaking up truth, getting prepared. But we also need to be *in the world.* In fact, as we've already noted, being in the Word is what prepares us for being in the world. But if we're in the Word all the time without having contact with the world, we'll drift into spiritual obesity. We'll become weighed down with heavy truths that we never put into practice. We'll lose our edge and our effectiveness.

On the other hand, if we're in the world all day long without adequate preparation in the Word, we'll end up conforming to our surroundings, lacking a sufficient standard of truth to counteract the incessant influence of the world. Unfortunately, most Christians lose this "double contact" (with the Word and the world) soon after their conversion experience. The sheer joy of coming to Christ and the thought of acceptance from a new group cause many to shift too far to one side. Soon we lose all close contact with the unbelieving world. Before long, all our friends are Christian friends; all our activities are Christian activities. Our old friends, the worldly ones we used to hang around with and who might really benefit from exposure to a Christian perspective, are cut off. "It's just too risky," we think. "After all, I was messed up when I was hanging around that crowd. I need to back off." But if we back off too far, our friends will never understand the life-changing transformation we have undergone. They'll never be drawn closer to God or learn how to be rescued themselves.

To thrive as disciples, we need spiritual food *and* exercise. We must be fed a consistent diet of God's truth found in the Scriptures. But we also need to exercise our faith before the unbelieving world. As we incorporate a consistent "workout program" of living authentic Christian lives in the midst of a fallen world, as we feed on truth and breathe heavenly breezes of regular prayer, we will grow stronger than ever. The world needs us as Christians, and we need the world. Jesus said that we're "the salt of the earth" (Matthew 5:13). But salt doesn't do any good sitting in the saltshaker; it must be emptied out. It's the same with our lives—we must pour ourselves out into the surrounding culture. By God's grace, it's possible to have contact without contamination.

On the northeastern seaboard of the United States, fishing is big business, and the demand for North Atlantic cod is always strong. This cold-water fish, valued for its meat, liver oil, and other products, resides near the bottom of inshore regions, as well as in deeper waters. Typically, when it was shipped to other regions of America, it was sent frozen. But people who were familiar with the Atlantic cod were dissatisfied, saying the fish lost much of its flavor in transit. The fishermen tried shipping live fish in tanks of seawater, but it was far too expensive, the flavor was still disappointing, and the meat was soft and mushy. Then someone who knew that the cod are migratory fish that compete for food along the ocean bottom suggested a different approach. The fish were placed in containers with their natural enemy, the catfish. The catfish would chase the cod around the tank from the time they left the East Coast until they arrived at their destination. The results were remarkable. The energy expended in running from the catfish left the cod fresh, firm, and flavorful!

There's something to be said for staying in contact with the world, even though it may get rough out there sometimes. It keeps us abreast of people's thoughts, ideologies, and feelings about life in general and about God in particular. It keeps us fresh and relevant. And it fulfills Christ's purpose in sending us into the world.

A friend told me about the news coverage he had seen of a tornado that had swept through the Midwest. A week after the storm had done its dastardly deed, one of the local newspapers followed up with this statement: "We're pleased to announce that the cyclone that blew away the church last Friday did no real damage to the town."

If it's true that the town didn't miss the church, how sad! Apparently those Christians had lost their flavor and had become irrelevant.

8

TALKING STRAIGHT
TO GOD

At that time you won't need to ask
me for anything. The truth is, you
can go directly to the Father and ask
him, and he will grant your request
because you use my name. You haven't
done this before. Ask, using my name,
and you will receive, and you will
have abundant joy.   John 16:23-24

❖ ❖ ❖

When my son Nathan was still quite young, I assured him
that he could always get an audience with me, no matter
how busy I was. Of course, he had to learn, as most pastors'
kids do, that his dad's life could get pretty busy and that
there were lots of time demands and people demands. But I

never wanted him to get lost in the shuffle and grow up feeling like a "second-class citizen."

When I told him he would always have access, I meant *always*. He could march into my office any time he was at church (no matter who else was in there). And he did. There were times when he'd strut proudly past secretaries, assistant pastors, and anyone else who might be there and barge in to Dad's inner sanctum. Sometimes it was to show me a drawing he'd made; other times he needed a couple of dollars for a snack; other times he had an "owie" he wanted me to see. No matter what the occasion, it was always an important one—to him! Others at times may have felt a bit put out by such intrusions, but they got over it. My son loved it. And so did I! What gave him such privileged access? One simple fact—he's my boy.

When Jesus was here on earth, the disciples had privileged access to him. They brought their requests and their questions directly to him. But as he prepared them for his imminent departure, Jesus revealed a new way for them to pray—talking directly to the Father. They could now come to God at any time and for any reason.

From Jesus' subsequent prayer to the Father, we can glean some other key principles to bolster our prayer lives—both for ourselves and for others. If you make this pattern a regular part of your communication with God, it will soon become second nature. I suggest that you learn to "talk straight" with God, using these three simple requests: *Keep me, Lord; Teach me, Lord;* and *Send me, Lord.*

⊡ ⊡ ⊡

KEEP ME, LORD

In the same way that Jesus asked his Father not to remove his disciples from the world but to keep them safe, I encourage you to pray for yourself, your Christian friends, your family, pastors, and leaders.

Thank God for your present position in life—your occupation, family, school, career, home, neighborhood, state, and country. Reflect on God's promises to you, such as those contained in the following verses:

> ✣ Romans 8:28: "And we know that God causes everything to work together for the good of those who love God and are called according to his purpose for them."
> ✣ Psalm 32:8: "I will guide you along the best pathway for your life. I will advise you and watch over you."
> ✣ Acts 17:26: "He decided beforehand which [nations] should rise and fall, and he *determined their boundaries*" (emphasis added).

God has placed you where you are for his own purposes. Thank him for all the blessings he has poured out on your life.

Tell God about the difficulties you experience living "in the world." Be honest about how you feel when other people—

whether it's your family, friends, or coworkers—criticize, ridicule, or question your faith. Tell him if you feel tempted to compromise or tone down your Christianity when others confront you or aren't sympathetic.

This was once a big issue for me. In two of the hospitals where I worked as a radiological technician, I experienced what seemed to me to be incessant ridicule from my colleagues. Some of it, I found out later, was rooted in jealousy that others felt about my personal work ethic, which was threatening to them. But much of it had to do with the intense dislike they had for spiritual things. Whenever I was around, their defenses went up, and I bore the brunt of it. In fact, several coworkers shunned me. It was an especially difficult time for me. I was tempted to compromise my firm spiritual convictions and settle into a more relaxed mode, not only publicly but personally as well. Instead of giving in to the world's system, however, I made it a subject of much prayer.

Ask God to keep you safe from the strong currents of evil that pressure you. Ask him to give you stamina, an attitude of endurance that will keep you resilient in the face of hostility. Submarine officers speak of a place they call "the cushion of the sea," a depth so far below the storms raging on the surface that even the mightiest squalls are virtually imperceptible. A tempest that would otherwise destroy a vessel on the surface doesn't affect a submarine sitting in the depths of "the cushion."

But notice that the submarine isn't taken out of the ocean—it finds its refuge and its purpose in the midst of the sea. Likewise, we must remain in vital contact with the world in order to be relevant and effective in reaching the lost.

Ask God to take you to a new depth of faith, where his love and mercy will keep you safe from the raging storms of life. Ask him to give you a "submarine faith" so that he becomes more real to you in times of trial. Listen to the psalmist's confident voice in the midst of the storm: "God is our refuge and strength, always ready to help in times of trouble. So we will not fear, even if earthquakes come and the mountains crumble into the sea . Let the oceans roar and foam. Let the mountains tremble as the waters surge!" (Psalm 46:1-3).

◈ ◈ ◈

TEACH ME, LORD

Don't forget that your Bible is part of your survival gear. It's the handbook God has given us to make us fit for his service. We need daily contact with the Scriptures to be prepared to face the world system. Hiding the Word of God in our hearts (Psalm 119:11) is the primary way for us to remain holy (set apart, consecrated to God). Pray *before* you read, asking God for insight into his truth; then pray *after* you read, asking God to help you apply his truth to your specific situation.

Rejoice that God has given you the truth. The Bible is a powerful resource. Jesus referred to the Scriptures as "your words of truth" (John 17:17). The more you know, the more you'll grow—and the better you'll pray as you become more aware of God's will. Don't think of Bible study as an inconvenience or a mandatory reading assignment. See it for what it is: your lifeline to standing firm in an unsettled environment. Think of how aimless you'd be without such a standard of truth. Thank God that he is willing to reveal to you his will, his ways, and his life. Concerning unbelievers David wrote, "Their hearts are dull and stupid, but I delight in your law" (Psalm 119:70). As we delight ourselves in God's Word, he will sharpen us and prepare us to face the world.

Reveal to God your desire to be holy. In prayer, tell him that you're committed to becoming a godlier person. Let him know that you are consecrating yourself to learn more about his Word so that you can better respond to him in obedience. Even if your situation in life is painful, tell him you trust him anyway. Learn to pray like David, who said, "The suffering you sent was good for me, for it taught me to pay attention to your principles. Your law is more valuable to me than millions in gold and silver!" (Psalm 119:71-72). Suffering is often the key that awakens our desire for holiness.

Request explicit direction. Ask God to reveal specific truths that pertain to your circumstances. As you read the Bible, search for promises and principles that apply to your life experience. You won't find these answers in the form of theological texts arranged systematically. Instead, you'll learn about God through the experiences of biblical characters, through poetry, prophecy, and precepts. The key is to read the Scriptures *through the specific lens of your situation.* Approach the Bible through the grid of who you are, where you live, where you work, and the other circumstances of your life. Examine the Scriptures *as they apply to your life experience,* and they will yield untold riches of wisdom and truth. David prayed, "Teach me your principles. Help me understand the meaning of your commandments, and I will meditate on your wonderful miracles" (Psalm 119:26-27). Peter tells us that the Scriptures provide "everything we need for life and godliness" (2 Peter 1:3, NKJV). The Bible is packed with life-giving direction. Once you uncover these principles, ask the Holy Spirit to bring these truths to mind at the proper time (John 14:26).

▨ ▨ ▨

SEND ME, LORD

Not only do we need spiritual food—in the form of biblical truth and understanding—we also need spiritual exercise to stay strong in our faith. God wants to use our place in the world and our knowledge of the Word to further his strategic purposes. Let this be part of your daily prayer: *Lord, use me today in some way to tell others about you. I want to be your ambassador just as Jesus was while he was here on earth.*

Ask God to make you willing. One of the greatest fears that many Christians have is the prospect of talking to someone about their faith. It can be intimidating, especially if your spiritual conversation happens to be with an articulate and intelligent atheist. But don't worry. You'll be surprised how well you'll be able to navigate the precarious waters of evangelism with God's help. You may also be surprised at how readily answers just seem to come to you while you are speaking. Jesus told his followers that even if they were imprisoned for their faith, God would still use them powerfully. "When you are arrested, don't worry about what to say in your defense, because you will be given the right words at the right time" (Matthew 10:19). Jesus wasn't downplaying the need to be adequately prepared through the study of God's Word; he was simply stating that God works in tandem with our minds to produce a powerful testimony before the world.

Ask God to make you ready for action. In a sense, you must relinquish your right to privacy in order to be available to God. You may be sitting next to someone on an airplane, standing in a long line at the grocery store, or eating in a restaurant when an opportunity arises for you to share God's truth. Don't be intimidated; simply ask God to give you the proper words, the proper tone, and the proper attitude to be an effective witness for him. You don't have to be obnoxious (in fact, it's much better if you're not) or stuff the truth down someone's throat. Just be willing and ready to share with others what God has shown you. Remember, it's not about *you,* it's about the hope that is in you—namely, the power of Jesus Christ to change people's lives. If you feel self-conscious, realize that it is a device of the enemy intended to distract and discourage you. Press on, and God will reward your persistent obedience.

Ask God to make you powerful. We are mortal beings doing immortal business, so we can't expect to be effective by ourselves. We need more than the "arm of flesh" to make an eternal impact. Evangelistic techniques may even get in the way of such spiritual work. Instead, rely on God's resources, especially the Holy Spirit. As Paul told the Corinthians, "We are human, but we don't wage war with human plans and methods. We use God's mighty weapons, not mere worldly weapons, to knock down the Devil's strongholds" (2 Corinthians 10:3-4). Jesus promised, "When the Holy Spirit has come upon you, you will receive power and will tell people about me everywhere—in Jerusalem, throughout Judea, in Samaria, and to the ends of the earth" (Acts 1:8). When you ask God to fill you with his Spirit, you can expect results. In your encounters with other people, you can be assured that God will use your gifts and abilities to further his purpose.

◈ ◈ ◈

COOPERATING WITH THE HEART OF GOD

What can we do to cooperate with God's desire to protect us, prepare us, and send us out into the world to accomplish his purpose? Let me suggest two vital decisions we must make: how we will respond to the world and how we will respond to God's Word.

Decide now how you will respond to the world.

When we declare our allegiance to God through faith in Jesus Christ, we can no longer remain neutral in the spiritual war that rages around us. We must decide how we will respond to the world. We have several options: isolation, insulation, stagnation, imitation, or permeation.

Isolation This is the monastic response. It's the "pillar philosophy" (remember Simeon Stylites?) that says we must escape our sinful environment in order to remain holy. However, isolation defeats God's purpose in placing us "in the world." Any good artist wants his work to be displayed—and God is no different. He wants his workmanship to be on display as well. "For we are God's masterpiece. He has created us anew in Christ Jesus, so that we can do the good things he planned for us long ago" (Ephesians 2:10). Isolation is not the best response; in fact, it's the very opposite of what God has in mind for us.

Insulation This is the response that says, "Okay, I know I have to live in the world, but I can pad myself and protect myself from all the problems and the pain. I'll just ignore it and pretend it's not there. I won't visit homeless shelters or watch the news about starving children in third-world countries." As long as the SUV is full of gas and the country club dues are paid, life is dandy for those who seek insulation. "Life's tough, but not in my backyard. As for all those unbelievers in my neighborhood, they better not get too close or I'll call the police!"

Stagnation This is a serious condition that indicates a spiritual malfunction. A stagnant Christian is like someone in a spiritual coma. The body continues to function at some level, but it's unconscious of the surrounding world! All the life and energy goes to preserving the system of Sunday morning worship, Wednesday night prayer, and occasional social gatherings and holiday celebrations, but there's no viable impact on the needs of the world. "After all," this person might say, "Jesus said, 'The poor you have with you always,' so what am I supposed to do? There will always be needy people out there."

Imitation When they find the strong current of the world's system too difficult to fight, some people decide to just go with the flow. They float downstream, going where sinners go, doing what sinners do, and hoping God understands. Some might even say, "Hey, in order to reach the world, we have to adopt the world's methods, become 'culturally relevant.' After all, didn't Paul say he had 'become all things to all men'?" But this response is like a leper who has been cured getting close enough to another leper to contract the disease again. There's a better way!

Permeation As we discussed in an earlier chapter, this response requires us to be *in* the world but not *of* it. Clearly, the world needs agents of change who are willing and able to operate inside the world system without being corrupted by it. The world desperately needs "permeating Christians." In one sense, we are its only hope. If we who know the truth (and thus bear the antidote to the world's disease) don't make meaningful contact with those around us who are suffering the ravages of sin, what hope do they have?

But how can we have a meaningful impact on the world when the situation seems so desperate and so overwhelming? Let me make a practical suggestion. Start by looking up an old friend with whom you've lost contact—or perhaps someone you deliberately severed contact with when you became a Christian. Either by letter, phone call, or in person, tell that person what has happened to you. You may want to remind him or her what you were like before you came to Christ. Explain your search for more and how you met Jesus Christ. Talk about the changes you and others have observed since you became a Christian. Ask God to help you remember key passages of Scripture that will shed light on your friend's situation and speak of the hope of heaven. Keep it simple and watch what happens. Whether your friend's response is hostile or favorable, either way you will have cooperated with Jesus' prayer to make you a "sent one" into the world he loves so much. You'll soon discover more doors of opportunity opening up for you to share your faith. You'll discover a whole new way of life as you go about your Father's business.

Decide now how you will respond to the Word.

God wants to keep you—and he promises he will. After all, Jesus prayed that you would be "kept," and God will certainly answer the prayer of his Son. But you must also want to be kept! The same writer who says, "All glory to God, who is able to keep you from stumbling, and who will bring you into his glorious presence innocent of sin and with great joy" (Jude 1:24), also says, "Keep *yourselves* in the love of God" (Jude 1:21, NKJV, emphasis added). We strike the right balance when we put ourselves in a place where God can do his maximum work and we can experience his maximum power. This is where our study of the Scriptures comes in.

Jesus said that God's truth is what readies us to face an antagonistic world. We must decide what role the Bible will play in our lives. Will we make the Scriptures a part of our daily schedule, or will they sit idly on the shelf between Sundays? Will we commit ourselves to a church and a fellowship class or discussion group where we can learn and apply God's truth, or will the truth remain like ore in a mine, never to be dug out and enjoyed? If we separate ourselves from the source of God's truth, the Bible, we risk giving in to the strong pressure to conform to the world (Romans 12:1-2). The Holy Spirit wants to make us holy, and he uses the Holy Bible to do it. Here's what Billy Graham says about being in the world but not of it:

> The Bible teaches that we are to live in this world, but we are not to partake of the evils of the world. We are to be separated from the world of evil. When I face something in the world, I ask, "Does it violate any principle of Scripture? Does it take the keen edge off my Christian life? Can I ask God's blessing on it? Will it be a stumbling block

to others? Would I like to be there, or reading that, or be watching that, if Christ should return at that time?" Worldliness doesn't fall like an avalanche upon a person and sweep him or her away. It is the steady drip, drip, drip of the water that wears away the stone. The world is exerting a steady pressure on us every day. Most of us would go down under it, if it weren't for the Holy Spirit who lives inside us, and holds us up, and keeps us.[1]

Feed yourself a steady diet of God's truth. Study the Bible in order to prepare yourself for service, and pray that God would show you someone who needs to hear the truth. Ask God for a challenge so that you'll grow in your faith. Remember, like the Atlantic codfish, it takes exercise to maintain your strength, your flavor, and your texture, and to avoid succumbing to a mushy, mediocre, bland spiritual life. This daily cycle of refueling and burning it off will accelerate your spiritual growth. Try it for a month and see if it doesn't supercharge your faith.

Part Three

A LOOK INWARD—

THE WHOLE CHURCH

UNIFIED

9

"THAT THEY WILL BE ONE"

Now I am departing the world; I am leaving them behind and coming to you. Holy Father, keep them and care for them—all those you have given me—so that they will be united just as we are. . . .

I am praying not only for these disciples but also for all who will ever believe in me because of their testimony. My prayer for all of them is that they will be one, just as you and I are one, Father—that just as you are in me and I am in you, so they will be in us, and the world will believe you sent me.   John 17:11, 20-21

❖　❖　❖

The air was moist with impending rain. As threatening clouds piled up above the outdoor venue, thousands of fans waited expectantly for the concert to begin. Lightning flashed in the distance and the glare of the stage lights played across the seats and the lawn that was now packed with people. At last, Ziggy Marley, the Grammy Award–winning reggae musician, sashayed onto the stage with his band. He came not only with a repertoire of catchy melodies to entertain but also with a message to preach—a message that would resonate deep in the hearts of his audience that night. It was a message of unity and world peace.

Since the death of his father, the legendary Bob Marley, Ziggy has carried on the tradition of self-styled music with a message, he claims, for the new millennium. It's a message laced with selective biblical imagery that resounds deeply with his fans. Marley touts the need for finding a spiritual path while insisting that all religions must be done away with since they are the cause of the world's ills.

"What we need is love," he insists, "not religion. People say they love God, but then they go out and blow up others who don't agree with them!"

The spectators cheered wildly as Marley preached and sang over the megawatt sound system. Although his pulpit is nontraditional—standing behind a microphone with a vintage Les Paul guitar—his congregation is both enthusiastic and loyal. Everyone wants world peace and everyone would love to see unity among the earth's inhabitants. It's a no-lose message that will never be met with rejection, especially in a culture desperately hungering for solutions to the wars and unrest in the world.

Marley's message also resonates with every Christian. We too want and expect to see world peace one day, when the Prince of Peace returns. But we are not naïve. Until that day, however, it's unrealistic to imagine that everyone on earth could simply shove aside his or her ideological differences, religious heritage, and personal enmities to embrace an ecumenical brotherhood. It's absurd! Why? Because we know that true brotherhood and sisterhood only comes from a blood bond. Our unity as Christians is the direct result of Jesus' death on the cross, which enables anyone from any culture at any time to be a part of God's family (Ephesians 2:14-18).

Of course, that's also the rub.

Anyone familiar with church history knows that Christians have not always been paragons of harmonious accord. Past and present is littered with examples of Christian groups playing theological tug-of-war and dividing over organizational and philosophical differences. Countless denominations and movements began as splinter groups from other congregations—and everyone is convinced, on both sides, that their own beliefs are purer and more biblical. Consequently, it's not surprising that today in America there are hundreds of denominations represented by more than 405,000 places of worship and more than 100,000 other worship centers with no affiliation to any other group.[1] We are a fractured people. Why should people of other religions be persuaded about the uniqueness of Jesus and the gospel when they see a torn and divided church? No wonder so many young people in the 1960s echoed a common refrain: "Jesus, yes! Christianity, no!"

How do we answer those who advocate spiritual unity and world harmony? How do we come to grips with the problems inside the church? Of course we want unity and a sense of oneness among God's people. As one Latin American theologian has said, "The proclamation of the gospel apart from the unity of the church is a theological absurdity."[2] He's right, but we must be careful not to confuse true unity with something far less pure and far more corrupting.

❖ ❖ ❖

TRICKLE-DOWN EVANGELISM

All of human history—past, present, and future—lies within the purview of Jesus. Throughout his life on earth, he frequently demonstrated his prophetic awareness. He foretold the destruction of the temple (Matthew 24:2), the writing of the New Testament (John 14:26; 16:13-15), a time of worldwide hardship (Luke 21:25-26), his coming again (Mark 13:24-27), and the future kingdom of heaven (Luke 21:31; 22:18). Jesus was as certain of the future as we are of the past.

In his prayer to the Father in John 17, Jesus again demonstrates his omniscience. As if looking through the telescope of the future, through the years of evangelistic outreach, Jesus anticipates the problems we observe to-day—discord and disunity. He anticipates the imperfection of his church. He sees the flaws, the factions, and the fragmentation. And in light of these, he prays for unity—that a sense of oneness would be discovered and enjoyed by all his followers.

Jesus' prayer takes an important shift at this point. He first prayed for himself (John 17:1-5) and then for his immediate disciples—those who had been with him in his earthly sojourn (John 17:6-19). Now Jesus looks ahead through the ages and prays for his future followers: "I am praying not only for these disciples but also for all who will ever believe in me because of their testimony" (John 17:20).

I am at once arrested and humbled by this revelation. It takes my breath away to realize that you and I were on the Savior's mind just a few hours before his sacrificial death on our behalf. As I consider this next section of Jesus' prayer, I look with anticipation to see exactly what he prayed concerning us.

Jesus foresees a spiritual momentum resulting from what his disciples will do once they are sent out into the world. He's obviously confident that God will grant his requests to keep the disciples safe from the evil one and to purify them and make them holy, and that their outreach to the world will be successful. That's implied by this change of focus in the prayer. Jesus sees that scores of people will respond to the disciples' message—and once they respond, they too will pass it along. Some will preach, others will write letters to the churches, and a few will write historical accounts of the life of Jesus. As a result, multitudes will come to believe. In effect, Jesus anticipates what has long been a hallmark of the Christian church: "trickle-down evangelism."

The eleven remaining disciples (after Judas's betrayal) went out and told others who lived in Jerusalem, then Judea and Samaria. Some who heard, including Saul of Tarsus, eventually believed the message and were converted. Then, because of the power of such a change, the message was passed along to others—and it has never stopped, down through the generations! Across two millennia, the stream of truth still flows with undiminished power, filling empty hearts in virtually every age and culture. Two thousand years later, here we are, reading the gospel penned by the apostle John, who was there the night Jesus prayed this prayer!

There's no telling how big and far-reaching an impact we might have if we're obedient to God's calling on our lives and we share the good news with even one other person. Consider the story of Edward Kimball.

Like most of us, Kimball had no idea how far trickle-down evangelism can travel. He was simply following God's call on his heart when he stepped inside a Chicago shoe store in 1856 to tell a young man about Jesus Christ. As it happened, the shoe salesman, whose name was Dwight L. Moody, listened to Kimball and received Christ as a result. He later attended Kimball's Sunday school classes.

Moody went on to become one of America's most beloved evangelists and pastors. Moody Memorial Church in

downtown Chicago and Moody Bible Institute bear an elo-
quent testimony to Edward Kimball's obedience to carry
the message to others. But it didn't stop there. Countless
thousands of others heard the gospel through the ministry
of Dwight L. Moody, and many more were inspired by his
life and preaching. One was J. Wilbur Chapman. A student
at Lake Forest College in the late 1870s, Chapman attended
one of Moody's evangelistic meetings in Chicago and after-
ward received some personal counseling from Moody.
Chapman later became a friend and coworker of Moody's.

Eventually Chapman, who worked with the YMCA,
hired a former major league baseball player named Billy
Sunday as his assistant and secretary. Soon Sunday started
preaching on his own. He spoke at army camps during
World War I and later held citywide meetings all over
America. So far, Edward Kimball's seed was bearing incredible and unexpected fruit! But that's just the beginning.

Billy Sunday's influence fanned the flame of evangelism
throughout the United States. His preaching in Charlotte,
North Carolina, in 1924 sparked the interest of local Christian businessmen, who formed a men's prayer and fellowship group, originally known as the Billy Sunday Layman's
Evangelistic Club. Their excitement led to the planning of a
crusade in 1934, featuring evangelist Mordecai Ham. On
the last night of the Charlotte crusade, a lanky young man
named Billy Graham walked forward and prayed to receive
Jesus Christ. And to think it all began with the simple witness of an ordinary Chicago Sunday school teacher named
Edward Kimball.[3]

This example of trickle-down evangelism shows the potential of one obedient disciple. Who knows what will happen if you and I continue the legacy of passing the gospel truth along to someone else. Give a man a dollar, and you cheer his heart. Give him a dream, and you challenge his heart. Give that man Christ, and you change his heart!

Yet the problem of disunity still persists. If our hearts are changed, why does Jesus need to ask the Father for unity? Has something happened to the church since the time of the disciples, or have Christians always had a difficult time getting along with each other?

❖ ❖ ❖

CAN'T WE ALL JUST GET ALONG?

Four times in his prayer, Jesus prays that his followers would be unified in love. To repeat a request so many times in so short a span means it must have been important to him. We can see in verse 23 that his request is anchored to a solid reason: "[That] the world will know that you sent me and will understand that you love them as much as you love me." In other words, a unified church will convince people that there is a God in heaven! It all makes sense, doesn't it? Christians are being watched closely by the scrutinizing eyes of the world. We preach the message of the gospel—that Jesus was sent into the world to be the solution for our sins—but the world is looking for any flaws that might discredit our claims. And they're only too quick to point out any hint of hypocrisy or any failure in the lives of Christians.

What does it mean to be united as Christians? Does it mean we'll agree about everything? Not likely. As the late apologist and theologian Walter Martin once told me, "If you find two people who agree on everything, one of them isn't thinking." So how can we be unifying *and* discerning? How do we work through honest differences in theology and style of worship to determine what is valid, yet at the same time promote harmony in the body of Christ? It's an important question because not everyone who names the name of Christ necessarily belongs to Christ (Matthew 7:21-23; 2 Timothy 2:19). Nor is every organization that claims to have a handle on the truth a true Christian church. Such a statement by its very nature is divisive, so how can we be thoughtful, discerning Christians who can distinguish between true and false theology while promoting love and unity?

First, let's admit that not everyone who is called a disciple in the Bible was a true follower. The most obvious example is Judas Iscariot. He went along with the crowd, but in the end he balked at Jesus' messianic claims and betrayed him to his enemies. There was also a whole group of disciples who decided not to follow Jesus once his preaching became controversial: "At this point many of his disciples turned away and deserted him" (John 6:66). And there was Simon of Samaria, a notable magician who "believed and was baptized." Yet Peter was adamant that his heart was "not right before God" (Acts 8:13, 21).

Next, let's recognize that many characters in the Bible didn't always agree with each other. We sometimes idealize people like Peter, Paul, and Barnabas, choosing to view them through the stained-glass window of time and tradition, but these esteemed leaders had their moments of disunity and dysfunction. The disciples argued on more than one occasion, including a vigorous debate about who would be the greatest in the coming kingdom—an argument that continued on the very night Jesus Christ prayed his prayer (Luke 22:24). Several years later, the apostle Paul confronted Peter about a seeming double standard that Peter had when he was with Gentile Christians. Their disagreement became public when the two met in Antioch (Galatians 2:11-16). In Acts 15:4-12, we see that some Christians in the early Church couldn't agree on the requirements for salvation! It took a church council to settle the matter. Paul and Barnabas were close friends until they had an argument that separated them for the rest of their lives! The contention was sharp, the words they exchanged were virulent, and the result was a severed friendship and evangelistic partnership (Acts 15:36-40).

What are we to think? What does Jesus mean when he prays that his followers be one? Was he praying for the impossible? In the next chapter, we'll look at two possible interpretations: that Jesus was praying for organizational unity or that he was praying for uniformity. As we'll see, neither view can be altogether correct.

10

LET'S GET IT TOGETHER

JUST AS YOU ARE IN ME AND I AM IN YOU,
SO THEY WILL BE IN US, AND THE WORLD
WILL BELIEVE YOU SENT ME.   JOHN 17:21

❖ ❖ ❖

*O*rganizational unity has been attempted at different times in church history. Most notably it appeared in the fourth century A.D. when the Roman emperor Constantine and others after him sought to centralize the Christian church into one body, covering all of Europe, under the leadership of a pope. By the Middle Ages, the church had become a fully unified organization, yet it was fraught with many problems. What it had gained in organizational unity it had lost in love and purity. It was economically strong but spiritually impoverished. It was outwardly united in government but internally corrupt and morally weak.

History records the dark exploits of the church during

those years of organizational cohesion, including such infamous episodes as the Crusades and the Inquisition. While a finely tuned ecclesiastical machine maintained law and order on the European continent, evangelism was conducted by the edge of the sword. Pogroms kept the infidels at bay while a strict hierarchy of bishops, friars, and cardinals maintained a fearful presence among the people. Such mistakes must not be repeated. An enforced oneness, wherein only one point of view is tolerated is not what Jesus intended when he prayed for unity. Neither was he envisioning the seemingly progressive idea proposed by Ziggy Marley and others that we all just get along. Pursuing unity by minimizing differences is both naïve and unattainable. To think that we can all "visualize world peace" and form one glorious and flawless humanity is a dangerous notion. Such idealism says, "If only we could get rid of denominations and create one superchurch, we'd be better off." Would we, really? If we were able to unite under one big umbrella of brotherly love, how would it help? It would only spread confusion about what the truth really is.

Jesus wasn't referring to *uniformity* when he prayed for unity. Have you ever noticed how different all the disciples were? John's personality was different from Peter's, and Thomas was unlike Andrew. The disciples also differed in their ministries, each following his unique calling to spread the gospel throughout Jerusalem, Judea, and Samaria. Jesus never intended for his followers to be homogenized—wearing the same clothes, same hairstyles, voting for the same candidates, and reading from the same version of the Bible. How shallow we are when we seek to strip people of their individualism when they come to Christ! One of the great joys of Christian fellowship is the diversity of personalities, interests, giftedness, and styles of worship and evangelism that thrive within the body of Christ.

Uniformity is boring! Generic spirituality is dull and lifeless! Although we must hold to the central core of historical essentials in the Christian faith, we can enjoy a glorious latitude in nonessential matters. We'll never agree on every point of doctrine, but we can debate them vigorously without dividing over them vehemently. Although I have strong convictions about the proper way to worship, dress, evangelize, and baptize, and firm beliefs about the second coming of Christ, I don't want to make everyone a clone of myself or my church. Variety is thrilling! Why can't there be unity and diversity at the same time? The vast nature of God demands it. No single Christian movement, denomination, or assembly could ever embody all of God's personality. I love what Chuck Smith wrote to sum up the role his church would fill in the Orange County area of southern California: "We are not a denominational church, nor are we opposed to denominations as such, only the over-emphasis of the doctrinal differences that have led to division within the body of Christ. . . . We believe worship of God is fruitful. Therefore, we look for his love in our lives as the supreme manifestation that we have truly been worshiping him."[1] In other words, stop trying to make everyone your clone. Seek rather to make everyone Christ's disciple.

✠ ✠ ✠

UNITED WE STAND,
DIVIDED WE'RE CRAZY!

Although neither uniformity nor organizational consistency equates with true Christian unity, we can't overemphasize the importance of fellowship with other Christians. I need you, and you need me. The issue is unity of heart, spirit, and purpose—it's more internal than external. Powerful preaching, brilliant programs, and mass rallies all have their place, but nothing will persuade the world more convincingly that there is a God in heaven than the evidence of Christian brothers and sisters who genuinely love each other. Preaching the gospel without demonstrating love is false advertising. God's purpose for us includes more than delivering us from the flames of hell and providing us a ticket to heaven. He adopted us into a large family that spans the generations, and he wants unity in his family. That's what Jesus prayed for—and what he bled and died for.

The unity that God desires for the body of Christ is based on a unity that already exists in heaven between the three persons of the Trinity. As Jesus noted in his prayer to the Father, "You are in me and I am in you." God doesn't have to manufacture unity between himself, his Son, and the Holy Spirit—they're already unified. What that means for us is that our unity already exists in one sense. Anyone who affirms and believes the truth about God, his Son, and his Spirit—and their plans—is already a part of this heavenly unity. Paul affirms this truth several times in his letters to the churches. For example, he writes to the church in Corinth, "Now there are different kinds of spiritual gifts, but it is the same Holy Spirit who is the source of them all. There are different kinds of service in the church, but it is the same Lord we are serving. There are different ways God works in our lives, but it is the same God who does the work through all of us" (1 Corinthians 12:4-6). We are already a part of the same spiritual family. We enjoy an essential unity on that basis alone. So in one sense, we've already arrived; in another sense, however, we must enter into that unity. Paul writes, "Do your best to preserve the unity which the Spirit gives by means of the peace that binds you together. There is one body and one Spirit, just as there is one hope to which God has called you" (Ephesians 4:3-4, TEV).

When we become a part of the family of God, we become part of a preexisting unity. But preserving that unity is an ongoing effort. God himself established the family of God. And like any family, we don't have control over who our brothers and sisters will be. And just as in our earthly families we have brothers and sisters whether we want to or not, we can't reject our fellow Christians just because they live in a different place, worship in a different way, or emphasize different aspects of the character of God. Our relationship as a family already exists. Once we discover and acknowledge our family connections, we must preserve them in the bond of peace (Ephesians 4:3).

Our unity is also based on the revelation of God that Jesus gave us: "*I have passed on to them the words you gave me; and they accepted them* and know that I came from you, and they believe you sent me. . . . Holy Father, keep them and care for them—all those you have given me—*so that they will be united just as we are* (John 17:8, 11, emphasis added). Our brothers and sisters in Christ are those who have accepted what Jesus has said. It is with them that unity in the church will be enhanced and strengthened. We won't achieve unity with just anyone. It's just not possible. In speaking to the Pharisees, Jesus himself made the distinction between those who were his brothers and others who were in league with "[their] father the Devil" (John 8:44).

Not everyone who goes to church is a child of God; not everyone we meet is our spiritual brother or sister. But those who receive the same Savior in the same way—by faith—are our brothers and sisters. I've experienced this genuine unity with God's people around the world—in China, India, the Middle East, and Europe. Although our languages and cultures were different, we knew instinctively that we were family. Would we all agree on issues like the proper mode of baptism? Probably not! Would we all see eye to eye on church membership, the Lord's supper, the Second Coming, and which version of the Bible to read from? No! But on essential matters of the gospel—Jesus' atoning death on the cross, his bodily resurrection, and salvation by faith through grace—we would all agree. Those are primary issues by which we can distinguish our brothers and sisters. We may debate nonessential issues, such as styles of worship and methods and rituals, but we agree not to divide over them. We may disagree, but we do so agreeably to promote the unity that Jesus prayed for.

I'm reminded of the story of a father who had four sons who quarreled incessantly. Sometimes the arguments were benign; other times they flared up into explosive confrontations. Although these disagreements between brothers were not unusual, their father knew the potential damage that unrestrained tempers could create. One evening after a particularly heated bout, the father told the boys to step outside. He picked up a stick from the ground and held it out to his oldest son. "Snap it in two," he said. The boy broke it easily, with hardly any effort. Then the man bent down and took two sticks, handed them both to his son and said, "Snap them both together." Again the eldest son broke the sticks, although this time he met with a little more resistance from the strength of the two sticks combined. The father continued to add sticks—three, then four, then five— each time instructing his son to break them while the other boys watched with curiosity. Eventually, when the eldest son tried to break seven sticks held together, he was unable even to bend them and gasped in defeat. The wise father then explained, "It's easy to fight among yourselves, but there is strength in unity. Anyone can overthrow you one by one. But if you stand united together, your combined strength will prevail."

When Christians stand together in unity, they bear living proof of the truth of the gospel. But when they splinter over frivolous and nonessential issues, observers have reason to doubt the validity of the gospel.

When a visitor to a mental institution found that only one guard was watching one hundred inmates, he was shocked. "Aren't you afraid that one day these patients could get their heads together, perhaps attack you, and then escape?" The security guard just smiled calmly and replied, "These folks are here for their very inability to get their heads together and work cooperatively." Very suggestive, isn't it? To preach the gospel without unity is insanity!

❖ ❖ ❖

PRAYING FOR UNITY

How then do we achieve unity? Follow the flow of Jesus' prayer. First, he establishes that his disciples are those who know God's truth and do it; he notes that they have received the truth about God and made it their own (John 17: 6, 8). He prays that his disciples will be kept from becoming like the world around them yet will love the people of the world enough to tell them this truth (John 17:14-18, 20). He also explains that the purpose of what he revealed to them was so that they could have love one for another (John 17:26). If we pull together this section of Christ's prayer, we can see several important truths:

1. If we love God, we will love God's truth.
2. If we love God, we will love the people of the world he created enough to tell them the truth of the gospel.
3. If we love God, we will love God's people, because that's how the people of the world will understand our message.

How can we pray in light of these truths? Let's take Jesus' words and let them inspire our communication with God the Father. I suggest three points of focus for our prayers:

1. Pray for unity with integrity.
2. Pray for unity within the family.
3. Pray for unity in practice.

Let's explore each of these briefly.

Pray for Unity with Integrity

We need to make sure that our unity is real, not a false and sloppy sentimentalism more reflective of "rock concert" theology. We must exercise discernment and pray for a greater depth of knowledge of God's truth. Ask God for his wisdom in distinguishing between the wheat of essential truth and the chaff of nonessentials.† The goal is to embrace a message that is both doctrinally pure and demonstrably true. Truth *and* love must prevail together.

Warning: It's easy to become self-righteous when we pray for unity. We justify ourselves by saying that our

† When I refer to the "essentials" of the gospel, I'm not suggesting that some truths are dispensable and unimportant. All truth is essential truth. I'm merely distinguishing between those truths that are essential for salvation—and thus for being a Christian—versus those that are not. The essentials include humanity's fallen nature and need for salvation; salvation by grace through faith; the nature of Jesus Christ as both divine and human, his virgin birth, vicarious atonement, bodily resurrection, and imminent return. The essentials also include our depravity and God's sovereign ability. Belief in these truths is what makes people Christians. Learning these truths will help us discern between authentic Christians and those who are simply masquerading.

interpretation of Scripture is the right one, without paus-
ing to consider that every camp within Christianity says the
same thing about their own perspective on truth. We tend
to magnify secondary, nonessential issues and thereby
burn bridges of communication with other Christians. It's
too risky to try to function outside the walls of our own
tradition.

Of course, some of the barriers are historical ones
erected long before we came along and paid for by the
blood of church fathers. Many of our positions are justifi-
able and defensible—but we must be careful about our attitude toward others. Christian groups are too often
negative and overly suspicious of one another. We believe
the worst about each other and refuse to listen to anything
that doesn't buttress our predisposed beliefs. We need to
pray for a new attitude toward the church of Jesus Christ.
We must repent of the bad attitudes we harbor and even
justify. We should ask the Lord to give us hearts of love and
a desire to understand others. We may debate such issues
as tongues, baptism, predestination, music, fashion, poli-
tics, the Sabbath, diet, demons, and scores of other entic-
ing and important subjects, but we must ask God for an
understanding heart large enough to accept as our brothers
and sisters other people who hold divergent viewpoints.
God promises to bless those who promote harmony: "Harmony is as refreshing as the dew from Mount Hermon that
falls on the mountains of Zion. And the Lord has pro-
nounced his blessing, even life forevermore" (Psalm
133:3).

Pray for Unity within the Family

Start by praying for your own family. Sometimes families are fractured by opposing theological viewpoints. Jesus even foretold sharp divisions in some families because of the gospel (Matthew 10:34-37). Pray for unity in your spiritual family—the church you belong to as well as the entire body of Christ in your city and nation. The strength of the early church lay in the fact that they stood "side by side, fighting together for the Good News" (Philippians 1:27). When differences surfaced, such as the factions that arose within the Corinthian church, Paul promptly corrected them (1 Corinthians 3:1-11). The early church was not a monolithic group with one central organizing head and substructures that followed the directives of the home office. In the first century, there were church assemblies scattered across Asia Minor, Syria, and Greece—different in personality and style but all professing the lordship of Christ, all a part of the body.

As part of your prayer for unity, come humbly to the cross in repentance. Repent for any lack of love you have shown in the past. Ask God to forgive you for the harsh words you've spoken and the entrenched positions you've taken about secondary concerns. Repent for what you have contributed to the divisiveness that has split the church. Disunity not only hurts other Christians, it also offends God. At the cross, see what it cost Jesus to secure not only our salvation but also our unity. It was the cross that destroyed the barriers of "us" versus "them."

Pray for spiritual renewal: When our love for Jesus is

renewed, our love for others will be renewed as well. It begins with Jesus and spills over to the rest of the church.

Pray for Unity in Practice

Pray together with other Christians for unity. It would be incongruous to pray for unity among God's people and do it alone. This is the time to break down the barriers and invite the participation of other Christians from other groups. Praying together will forge bonds of mutual trust and genuine community. Praying together recognizes our deep need for one another. If you're a church leader, call a leader from another church and start there. Barriers within the body are often strongest at the level of leadership—and it's at that level they must be broken. If you serve on a committee that has a counterpart in another local assembly, get together for prayer. It will do wonders for both churches. Praying together will help to diminish any sense of competition that exists and will open up opportunities to share ideas. Practicing unity may start a chain reaction in your community. You may begin to see a softening of differences between other churches. As you meet to pray, God will be actively involved and answering your prayers.

Begin your first prayer time by announcing your intentions for unity. Agree not to speak (or pray) negatively about your church or other churches in the community. Agree that you won't try to solicit members from other churches (what have we come to?), but seek to strengthen the commitment of everyone to the body of Christ.

Initiating corporate prayer across church lines will take

some extra effort. No doubt you're already busy, maybe even overextended. But ask yourself, Isn't it worth it to see spiritual vitality return to the body of Christ? Isn't it worth it to see old wounds healed? How will we as Christians ever be able to love the lost or love our enemies as Jesus commanded unless we love each other first? The apostle John, who was an eyewitness to Christ's prayer that night, later wrote, "If we love our Christian brothers and sisters, it proves that we have passed from death to eternal life" (1 John 3:14). Praying together is one good way to demonstrate our unity. Remember, it was Jesus who requested that we get it together!

11

BUILD BRIDGES,
DON'T BURN THEM

A mother took her three-year-old daughter to church for the first time. The church lights were lowered, and the choir came down the aisle carrying lighted candles. All was quiet until the little girl began to sing in a loud voice, "Happy birthday to you, happy birthday to you . . ."

Some of our church practices and distinctions aren't easily understood by outsiders—whether they're unbelievers or simply from a different theological background. What's typical for one group of Christians may feel foreign to another. For those accustomed to a formal church environment, for example, candles are a commonplace element in worship. But to a three-year-old, candles mean someone is having a party! Both may be right when the situation is viewed from their perspective; but probably neither can immediately grasp the other's point of view.

As we seek to bring about unity within the body of Christ, we must be realistic. We're not going to change the whole Christian world overnight. Some ships turn slowly, and change often meets with resistance. In fact, churches are notorious for their resistance to change. Still, we can be agents of healing to the broken body of Christ on earth. We can persist in building bridges rather than burning them. Through our obedience to the call of Christ, we can cooperate with Jesus' prayer for unity.

※ ※ ※

BE AWARE

The body of Christ is much bigger than our local church fellowships. We need to raise our sights and seek to unify the whole church, not just the Christian assemblies in our city or nation. In Galatians 3:28 Paul writes, "There is no longer Jew or Gentile [perhaps we could add "or Baptist, Methodist, Presbyterian, or Pentecostal"], slave or free, male or female. For you are all Christians—you are one in Christ Jesus."

We need to become aware of the diversity within the church at large and begin to appreciate the unique contributions of various groups and individuals to the Lord's work, throughout history and around the world. We must listen to one another and try to understand each others' point of view. We're part of an intricate and colorful tapestry, woven through the ages. By reading church history and making ourselves aware of how God is working throughout the world today, we'll be able to see how our thread connects to the historic and essential Christian gospel. We'll also gain a deeper understanding of what is essential and what is not.

❖ ❖ ❖

BE HUMBLE

Paul's direction to the Philippians is a helpful guideline: "Don't be selfish; don't live to make a good impression on others. Be humble, thinking of others as better than yourself" (Philippians 2:3). When I remind myself that Jesus died for other people from other churches as well as for me, I'm humbled by the enormity of his saving grace. Seeing others as blood-bought children of God produces a humility that is essential to unity. We must humbly refuse to let animosity over petty issues separate us from our brothers and sisters in Christ.

On important doctrinal points, it's okay to have an opinion—even a strong opinion. It's even acceptable to debate the issues. But we must lay down our swords of bitterness and anger. Remember, our real enemy is the devil, not other Christians. We mustn't expend vital energy that will render us weak when we step into a bona fide spiritual battle!

❖ ❖ ❖

BE HELPFUL

In his instruction to the Philippians about unity, Paul writes, "Don't think only about your own affairs, but be interested in others, too, and what they are doing" (Philippians 2:4). Here's where unity becomes very practical and down-to-earth. Are there any projects at your church that you could be a part of? Do other churches in your area have needs that your church could meet? Sometimes our youth group will organize a work day at one of the smaller churches in town. They'll go out to serve these churches by cleaning their buildings, painting trim, pulling weeds to spruce up the outside appearance, and simply encouraging those in leadership. This display of helpful love makes Christianity "smell good" to other people. As Paul writes in 2 Corinthians 2:14, "Wherever we go he uses us to tell others about the Lord and to spread the Good News like a sweet perfume." The sweet scent of helpfulness is much more pleasant than the bitter smell of divisiveness. Tertullian, the early church historian, remarked that the pagan world's reaction to the early Christians was at first one of suspicion. After sending spies to view these first assemblies, their reaction was, "Behold, how they love one another!"

◈ ◈ ◈

BE PRACTICAL

As I mentioned above, I encourage you to find ways to interact with members of other congregations. You may want to meet with a small group of believers from other churches. The dynamics of such a group can be compared to a greenhouse. Plants can grow in a variety of places, but when the temperature, soil, hydration, and air pressure are all presented in a controlled environment, growth is maximized. I think you'll discover that your spiritual maturity will accelerate in such an environment of diverse believers.

It will help you forge your own beliefs more solidly, and it will enhance your understanding and compassion for others. It will broaden your view of the body of Christ.

❖ ❖ ❖

BE REASONABLE

Regardless of whether you're a Presbyterian, Baptist, Methodist, Episcopalian, Catholic, Pentecostal, or nondenominational independent, the question remains the same: Are you truly born again? Have you been spiritually born into God's family? Are you pursuing a vital and genuine relationship with Jesus Christ? Léon Joseph Cardinal Suenens, the archbishop of Mechlin-Brussels, Belgium, once said, "I believe that the solution of ecumenical disunity will not finally be the result of a dialogue between the Church of Rome and the Church of Canterbury or the Church of Moscow. It will not be a dialogue between the churches as such. It will be a dialogue between Rome and Jesus, Canterbury and Jesus, Moscow and Jesus, so that we can become more and more united in him."[1] It matters little which door you enter on Sunday mornings if you haven't yet entered through the door of Jesus Christ. Only when your heart is united with him in salvation can you be united with his spiritual children. Are you trusting in your tradition rather than in him? Is it possible that you've followed the stream of religious heritage passed down from your parents but you're unsaved? If so, then be reasonable rather than resistant to change: "'Come now, and let us reason together,' says the Lord, 'Though your sins are like scarlet, they shall be as white as snow; though they are red like crimson, they shall be as wool'" (Isaiah 1:18, NKJV).

We don't have to compromise love for the sake of truth, nor truth for the sake of love. Both are meant to dovetail perfectly together. The closer we walk with Christ, the more naturally we will be united with our spiritual brothers and sisters.

You may have heard the saying that "Jesus called us to be 'fishers of men,' but instead the church has settled for being 'keepers of the aquarium.'" The truth is, we can and should do both. We mustn't neglect the aquarium (the church) while trying to reach the world for Christ. To do so would be poor stewardship and a bad witness to the world. In fact, it's the unity within the aquarium that lends credibility to the gospel in our outreach to the world. However, if we want to preserve unity within the body of Christ, we can't major on the minors.

Every fall, when the geese head south for the winter, these predictable flying wonders travel together in a V formation. We've all noticed this, but do you know why they fly this way? As each bird flaps its wings, it creates an updraft for the bird immediately behind it. By flying in a V formation, the whole flock together can fly 71 percent farther than if each bird flew on its own. Whenever a goose falls out of formation, it suddenly feels the drag and resistance of trying to go it alone and quickly gets back in line to take advantage of the lifting power of the bird immediately in front. When the lead goose gets tired, it rotates back in the formation and another goose takes over the point position. The geese honk from behind to encourage those up front to keep up their speed. If a goose gets sick or is wounded by a gunshot and falls out of formation, two other geese will fall out and follow him down to help and protect him. They will stay with the wounded goose until it is either able to fly or it dies. Then the geese will launch out on their own or join another formation to catch up with their original group.

That's a great example for Christians, isn't it? Who should have the greatest sense of direction and love for a common purpose if not the church? With all the opposition we face and pressure from the world, we could sure use the mutual "updraft" and encouragement of one another. (This puts a whole new spin on the slogan "Honk if you love Jesus!") The key is to "stay in formation." Minor differences may exist between us. That's fine as long as we keep the major goal in focus. If people outside the church knew that we would stand by them and encourage them like a flock of geese in flight, they'd be busting the walls down to get in![2]

Part Four

A LOOK FORWARD—

THE INGLORIOUS

GLORIFIED

WHERE ARE YOU GOING?

FATHER, I WANT THESE WHOM YOU'VE GIVEN
ME TO BE WITH ME, SO THEY CAN SEE MY
GLORY. YOU GAVE ME THE GLORY BECAUSE YOU
LOVED ME EVEN BEFORE THE WORLD BEGAN!

O RIGHTEOUS FATHER, THE WORLD DOESN'T
KNOW YOU, BUT I DO; AND THESE DISCIPLES
KNOW YOU SENT ME. AND I HAVE REVEALED YOU
TO THEM AND WILL KEEP ON REVEALING YOU. I
WILL DO THIS SO THAT YOUR LOVE FOR ME MAY
BE IN THEM AND I IN THEM.   JOHN 17:24-26

❖ ❖ ❖

When cancer comes to call, life takes on a new perspective.
Reality crystallizes into unmistakable priorities. I've seen
many come to faith in Christ during such periods of pain and
treatment. Tony was different. It didn't seem to move him

that way. He was concerned, but not about spiritual matters. He was alarmed, but not for his eternal soul.

I didn't know Tony very well. I met him at the request of his mother, who lived in the mountains of North Carolina. Like all good moms, she was worried about her son; with Tony she had good reason. He was spiritually lost and displayed no interest in God whatsoever. I'd also heard about him from Franklin Graham, his boyhood friend, who had seen the kind of trouble Tony could get into, including some big-time drug dealing as well as involvement in an assassination plot against Cuban dictator Fidel Castro.

His mother figured that because Tony and I lived in the same town (Albuquerque), I could make a difference. After all, I *am* a minister. So I called him. He returned none of my calls. I called again. No response. Finally after several months, Tony's mother came to visit him and arranged a meeting over dinner. Tony and I met. We conversed politely. I invited him to church. He smiled. We shook hands and departed. *That's that,* I thought. *I'll probably never see that guy again.* I was wrong.

Tony didn't make contact for a long time, and several months passed before our paths crossed again. In the meantime, I had decided to call a friend who worked as an agent with the Drug Enforcement Administration to see if he could tell me anything about Tony. "Stay away from that guy," he advised. "He's got a long history and we've been pursuing him." But God had other plans. He too was pursuing Tony.

One day Franklin Graham called me. He was coming to

Albuquerque to speak at my church, and he wanted to know if I would invite Tony to come hear him. When I called Tony, he hesitated, as if dragging his feet as long as he could before making a commitment. But eventually he agreed to come, and he brought his son. The two heard Franklin's message and his appeal to come to Christ, but neither one responded. After the service Franklin spoke candidly and bluntly to Tony in my office about spiritual things. Displaying the resolve of a captured soldier unwilling to betray his country, Tony steadfastly refused to surrender to Jesus. "I'll be fine," he insisted. "I don't need that stuff!" But his resistance didn't last.

A few months later, I was standing over Tony's bed in a local hospital. When he looked up at me, I could tell things were different. I hadn't seen him in this condition before. He was weak, discolored, disquieted—and for the first time, very interested in what I had to say. The cancer had spread fiercely and was wreaking havoc on the body of a man who once had been more physically fit than most men his age. He was now weak and spoke in slow, deliberate, gasping sentences. I knew I had to talk to him again about spiritual matters. Time was a fading commodity and we both knew it.

Tony listened once more to the age-old story of God's love and willingness to forgive. He heard once again about the promise of life after death and a place called heaven that awaited him if he would only choose to go there. But again he resisted, this time unveiling the reason his heart was so opposed.

"You don't understand, Skip," he said. "You don't know what kind of a man I am; you don't know what I've done in my past, where I've been."

Tony wasn't aware of how much I *did* know about him, although I didn't know all the details. I knew he'd been a scoundrel. I knew he'd walked in some pretty sketchy company and been involved in dark and unlawful activity. But I also knew that he needed to find the peace only afforded by God's forgiveness.

"Tony, let me tell you a quick story about a guy you may be able to relate to. I don't know his name, but he was dying, like you are. In fact, he hung next to Jesus on another cross." I began to tell Tony about the thief on the cross, who, in his last moments of life, cried out to Jesus, "Remember me when you come into your kingdom!" Here was a guy facing the death penalty for a lifetime of deeds against the Roman government, asking for forgiveness with his last few dying breaths. Tony's eyes fastened onto mine as I recounted Jesus' firm response to the man: "I assure you, *today you will be with me in paradise.*"

For the first time, Tony was visibly touched. His eyes welled, tears bathing his pallid face. "That's the most beautiful thing I've ever heard," he said, his voice gravelly and broken by sobs. "Jesus forgave a man who spent his whole life doing wrong!"

"Yes! And he did it instantly, Tony," I quickly added. "Jesus promised that man heaven because he placed his trust in him. You can too, Tony. You *must,* and you must do it soon!"

"I will—" Tony's voice trailed off, his parched lips giving out airy tones. His battle with cancer would soon be over.

Two days later, Tony died. His mother later told me that he had made peace with God—the God he had resisted all his life. Cancer won the battle for Tony's life on earth, but Jesus won the war for Tony's eternal soul.

His funeral was small, with mostly family members attending, but it was filled with hope rather than despair. Tony's son understood where his father had gone. Tony's mother now realized God's purpose in allowing such a ravaging disease to take the life of her son. And I realized that Jesus will do just about anything to reach people, forgive them, and grant them a place in heaven to be with him forever. Jesus loves to glorify even the inglorious!

❖ ❖ ❖

LOOKING HOMEWARD

What do you have to look forward to? When your earthly sojourn is over, after a lifetime of serving Jesus (or after a few days, as in Tony's case), then what? After all the praying, worshiping, witnessing, temptation fighting, Bible reading, church going, and pain enduring, what's next? Where will we end up and how does our destination affect us right here, right now?

This brings us to Jesus' final words in his prayer to the Father. After praying for himself, his close friends, and his future followers, he once again looks homeward. Thinking of the future glory that awaits him and not wanting to be there without his friends and followers, Jesus prays, "Father, I want these whom you've given me to be with me, so they can see my glory. You gave me the glory because you loved me even before the world began!" (John 17:24). This brings the prayer full circle. Jesus began by longing for the glory he remembered enjoying in eternity past. Now he is asking that we—his followers—can experience it, too.

Jesus' prayer gives us a new perspective on death—it puts a new face on an old enemy. Humanity has long dreaded the inevitability of death. And yet if death is the gateway to glory, why should we fear it? There are obvious reasons, of course, such as missing loved ones and the feelings of emptiness we experience when they're not with us. But Charles Spurgeon, the exquisite communicator of Victorian London, suggests that death is actually a safeguard against being stuck here on earth:

> Do you know why the righteous die? Will I tell you what kills them? It is Christ's prayer in this verse [John 17:24]. It is that which fetches them up to heaven. They would stop here, if Christ did not pray them to death.[1]

Pastor Warren Wiersbe writes, "Every time a Christian dies, this prayer of Jesus is answered, because the soul of every Christian goes to heaven."[2] This is exactly what Jesus taught his disciples to look forward to. Knowing they were fearful of his leaving, he reassured them of his purpose and plan: "Don't be troubled. You trust God, now trust in me.

There are many rooms in my Father's home, and I am going to prepare a place for you. If this were not so, I would tell you plainly. When everything is ready, I will come and get you, so that you will always be with me where I am" (John 14:1-3). The certainty of his promise calmed their frayed and uncertain nerves. Later that same evening, Jesus asks the Father specifically for what he has already promised his disciples.

We might also remember that Jesus instructed the disciples to pray for their future glory *themselves,* when he responded to their request to teach them how to pray. In the prayer recorded in Matthew 6, commonly known as the Lord's Prayer, Jesus teaches the disciple to pray, "May your Kingdom come soon" (v. 10). We don't know exactly what Jesus meant by "soon." But ever since, disciples of Christ have been praying and longing for heaven to come. A few of Jesus' disciples had actually *seen* a preview of heaven's coming attractions. Peter, James, and John had been on the Galilean mountaintop when Jesus was momentarily transfigured gloriously. "As the men watched, Jesus' appearance changed so that his face shone like the sun, and his clothing became dazzling white" (Matthew 17:2). Jesus had allowed them to dip their fingers in the future and taste a few moments of the coming glory!

Eventually, either when we die or when Jesus returns for his church, we're headed for glory. That's the climax of all earthly history, when the kingdoms of this world become the kingdom of our Lord and of his Christ (Revelation 11:15). John, who was there on the night Jesus prayed and also on the Mount of Transfiguration, later caught another glimpse of glory from a lonely, rocky island in the Aegean Sea. He saw a vision of the glorified Christ and described him by saying, "Standing in the middle of the lampstands was the Son of Man. He was wearing a long robe with a gold sash across his chest. His head and his hair were white like wool, as white as snow. And his eyes were bright like flames of fire. His feet were as bright as bronze refined in a furnace, and his voice thundered like mighty ocean waves" (Revelation 1:13-15). Moreover, John pictured heaven's luminescence by saying, "The city has no need of sun or moon, for the glory of God illuminates the city, and the Lamb is its light" (Revelation 21:23). John capped his account of the revelation by praying, "Amen! Come, Lord Jesus!" (Revelation 22:20).

◈ ◈ ◈

THE WINDS OF CHANGE ARE BLOWING

When Jesus says "I want" in his closing comments, he uses a very strong word that means to be steadfastly resolved or determined. In asking that his disciples be with him, he was declaring his fixed purpose. What a great thought! Jesus will never rest satisfied until the spiritual communion that began with him on earth is completed in heaven! And because the Father always answers the prayers of his Son (John 11:42), we are assured that this resolute and determined desire of Jesus will be answered as well.

Of course, in order for that to happen, things are going

to have to change. *We* will have to change, because there's no way we could handle the future glory in our present state. When Moses asked to see God's glory, God countered, "You may not look directly at my face, for no one may see me and live" (Exodus 33:20). Because someday we will see him face-to-face and will live forever, change is inevitable.

Part of the answer to Christ's prayer will be physical changes that take place in us. Some of us will die and our spirits will instantly be taken to be with Christ to await the resurrection of our physical bodies. Others will have the incredible opportunity of being alive at the Rapture, the coming of the Lord for his church, and will experience an instantaneous physical change. Paul writes, "Let me tell you a wonderful secret God has revealed to us. Not all of us will die, but we will all be transformed" (1 Corinthians 15:51). Either way, there will be resurrection for every believer. That change will be necessary for us to handle the glory that lies ahead in the uncharted territory of the future. As John writes, "We can't even imagine what we will be like when Christ returns. But we do know that when he comes we will be like him, for we will see him as he really is" (1 John 3:2).

Once that change occurs and we are resurrected, that's when the fun really begins. We will be fully equipped to handle the atmosphere and topography of heaven. We will be with Christ, sharing his glory and living out the answer to his prayer. Even with all the imagery of the book of Revelation and the teachings of Jesus and Paul, we still find it difficult to imagine this thoroughfare to our future. John

MacArthur whets our appetite as he sums up what we have to look forward to:

> At the rapture, Christ will come to meet his redeemed citizens and to call them out of the earthly kingdom in preparation for his soon-coming rule. They will come into his presence, but instead of immediately returning, they will wait seven years while Christ conquers the remaining enemies on his earthly domain (Revelation 6–19).
>
> At his second coming, he will complete the victory and return with his redeemed citizens to consummate the kingdom. The saints of heaven and the redeemed of earth will then rule and reign with the Lord God Almighty as his priests for a thousand years (Revelation 1:6; 20:6).
>
> Revelation tells us it will be a thousand-year kingdom, in which he will set things right and rule with a rod of iron, and the world will finally hear the answer to the Lord's prayer that the universal kingdom become the earthly kingdom.
>
> The world will see Jesus Christ reigning here, when the curse is reversed and this earth is like God meant it to be before the Fall.
>
> Jesus is coming again.[3]

Lifelong disciples and last-minute converts (like Tony and the thief on the cross) will be there to share in the glory.

Christian missionaries who have sacrificed their lives on earth will experience the reward of their labors. What a day it will be! What a reunion! What a worship service! And the day will last forever! The inglorious will be glorified and forever changed—and we will see Jesus' glory forever!

13

WHAT WILL HEAVEN BE LIKE?

*Y*esterday morning I called a friend of mine in Beirut, Lebanon, named Sami Dagher. He is one of God's finest servants in the Middle East. Not only has he pastored an evangelical church there for many years, but he has also established a medical clinic in Sidon to treat Palestinians who would otherwise receive little care. I called Sami to encourage him during a very difficult time in his ministry.

The previous week, Bonnie Witherall, a thirty-one-year-old American missionary who worked at Sami's clinic, answered a knock on the door, unaware that she was opening the door to her own eternity.

When Bonnie unlocked the door and opened it, a man holding a 9 mm pistol fired three consecutive shots into her face and chest. The assassin was a religiously motivated zealot who claimed the clinic was too evangelically Christian for such an Islamic area. Bonnie's martyrdom was meant to send a strong message to Sami and others like him—*Stay out!*

But Sami isn't about to quit. He told me over the phone that he had just come back from Sidon after preaching at Bonnie's memorial service. Other pastors had told him not to go. "It's too dangerous, Sami. You mustn't risk your life or the work." He went anyway and preached to more than six hundred local leaders, clerics, and officials, some of whom may have been responsible for Bonnie's murder.

Believing that the Lord had arranged these circumstances, Sami preached, and he preached hard.

"If you hear that I have been killed," he told me, "don't you shed even one tear for me, because I will be in glory with my Jesus!"

I was silent. I knew that Bonnie was in heaven, and she was more alive now than ever before. But now my friend was telling me that he could be going there too—very soon. He was as bold as a lion and not ready to back down. He wanted to live his life to the fullest because if heaven awaited him, what did he have to lose?

I wonder how often you think about your eternal future. What kind of a grip does heaven have on the way you live—right here and now?

The journey to heaven begins with an *internal* change—a change of heart by which we become related to God spiritually (John 1:12). Next, a change of behavior occurs—a *moral* change from darkness to light that becomes evident as we grow in our relationship with God (Acts 26:18). Finally, there will be a *physical* change, from our present body into our resurrected body (1 Corinthians 15:20-28).

Change. Change. Change. It was Bonnie Witherall's

legacy, and it is our legacy as children of God. Change will fuel our prayer lives like nothing else.

But before we consider how our future glory can affect the way we pray today, let's first take a glimpse at what heaven—our final destination—will be like. When Jesus prayed that we would see his glory, what was he envisioning in his mind's eye? Understanding more about heaven will help us prepare for it while we're still living here on earth.

❖ ❖ ❖

HEAVEN WILL BE A PLACE OF VARIETY

As we've already seen, Jesus described heaven as a place having "many rooms" or mansions—places for us to live. In other words, heaven will be a place of variety and there will be room enough for everyone. It will be huge. John describes one aspect of heaven, the future city of New Jerusalem, as cubical in shape, but it's a cube of 1,400 miles (Revelation 21:15-16)—roughly the distance between Maine and Florida on all sides. That's a big city!

The diameter of the moon is approximately 2,160 miles; the New Jerusalem will be 2,600 miles in diameter. Think of it—a city shaped like a cubed skyscraper, whose dimensions are as high and as wide as they are long, with a diameter larger than the moon. To put it another way, the New Jerusalem will be around 2,250,000 square miles, or fifteen thousand times the size of London, England! Someone estimated that twenty billion people could inhabit such a city. Assuming that 25 percent of the city is used for dwelling places (just to pick a number) and the rest for streets, parks, public buildings, and common areas, it's possible that each person will have a "cubical block" measuring 75 acres on each face to call their own. From the description given by John in Revelation, this future town seems to have streets running vertically as well as horizontally so that travel is multidimensional. And that's only one aspect of our future glory. There will also be the millennial kingdom, a new heaven and a new earth—with plenty of things to do and places to see!

◈ ◈ ◈

HEAVEN WILL BE PERSONAL

In the upper room before Jesus prayed, he told his disciples that he was "going to *prepare a place*" for them (John 14:2, emphasis added). Heaven is a place that has us in mind. It is a place prepared by God for us to be with him. We will be changed to suit our new environment and the place itself will be decorated for our enjoyment. God created the earth in six days. It is magnificent. He fashioned the earth's biosphere with its variety of plants and animals. He balanced our atmosphere with the perfect blend of oxygen, nitrogen, and other gases. He did it all in six days and could've done it in a microsecond if he had chosen to. Now think of what heaven will be like—a place *prepared* for us since Jesus made his promise two thousand years ago. I wonder what heaven must look like by now!

✦ ✦ ✦

HEAVEN WILL BE A PLACE OF RELATIONSHIP

Jesus referred to the future place of his glory as "my Father's home." He didn't call it heaven. That's what we call it in English. The word is based on an old Anglo-Saxon term, *heofon,* meaning to be lifted up. But when Jesus spoke of heaven that night, he referred to it in relational terms. In heaven, we will be with our Father, our Savior, and our Helper, the Holy Spirit, in an immediate and intimate way.

Another way to think about heaven is in terms of the difference between a *house* and a *home.* It isn't the building itself or the furniture that makes a house a home, it's the *people* we live with that make it wonderful.

Heaven will be a place of variety and that makes it inviting. Heaven will be personalized and that makes it exciting. And because in heaven we will see and experience the close fellowship and glory of Jesus Christ, it will be a *uniting* place. I can't wait to be united with Jesus face-to-face. I also look forward to seeing others like Peter, Paul, Thomas, Abraham, and my friend Tony, who got in just in time! Heaven was Bonnie Witherall's hope, and it is a very real anticipation for Sami Dagher.

Charles Spurgeon used to tell his students, "When you speak of heaven, let your face light up. When you speak of hell—well, then your everyday face will do."[1]

⬚ ⬚ ⬚

WHAT DO WE DO NOW?

It's one thing to think about heaven from time to time; it's quite another thing to actually be affected by it in our life on earth. Obviously, Jesus wanted the thought of future glory to make a difference to us because he makes it the capstone of his prayer: "O righteous Father, the world doesn't know you, but I do; and these disciples know you sent me. And I have revealed you to them and will keep on revealing you. I will do this so that your love for me may be in them and I in them" (John 17:25-26). In other words, outsiders may not know God or care about heaven. But his followers *do* know God and *should* care about heaven. So what can we do to build up our interest in our future home? Let's answer a few questions.

How real is heaven to you?

Most people don't think much about heaven until somebody they know dies and they attend a funeral. Suddenly, the thought of heaven moves to center stage. But Jesus talked about heaven all the time. It was real to him and he wants it to be real to us. Let me suggest a few ways to make heaven more real in your thinking.

Learn about your future home. Take time to read the biblical descriptions of heaven. (See, for example, Acts 7:55-60; Hebrews 9:23-24; Matthew 18:10; Luke 15:10; 1 Corinthians 15:35-58; 2 Corinthians 5:8; Philippians

1:21-23; 1 Thessalonians 4:17; 1 John 3:2; and Revelation 4–5; 20–22.) The descriptions of heaven in these passages suggest that heaven will certainly not be boring—nor will it be quiet! As you read, place yourself in the scene. Notice your surroundings and what you hear. Notice also the descriptions of glory that these authors write about. It's helpful to look up and meditate at length on these descriptions of heaven.

Take a flight of imagination. Another thing I've found helpful is to go out into the country, far from the city lights, and pray. Go for a weekend campout if you can, but even a long walk or a stargazing trip will suffice. As you look up, think about where you are and what you are seeing. You live on a speck of dust (comparatively speaking) in a galaxy known as the Milky Way. It is one of millions of galaxies. In fact, there may be as many as 100 billion other galaxies besides ours! The Milky Way is pretty impressive in its own right. Its dimensions are approximately 10,000 by 100,000 light-years. What does that mean? Well, let's take an imaginary trip.

Imagine yourself strapped to a beam of light. Because light travels at 186,000 miles per second, you would be able to move quickly around the universe. If you could travel at that speed, you could circle planet Earth seven-and-a-half times in one second. If you launched outward, you would zip past the moon in $1\frac{1}{2}$ seconds. Two minutes and eighteen seconds later, you'd reach the planet Venus. After only $4\frac{1}{2}$ minutes, you would already be at Mercury, and at the $7\frac{1}{2}$ minute mark you'd reach the Sun. A four-hour flight would take you out to Pluto, and if you stayed aboard your flight for 4.3 years you'd reach the nearest star to the Sun, known as Alpha Centauri (25 trillion miles from Earth).

If you were to stay put on your beam of light whirling through space at 186,000 miles per second, it would take you 100,000 years to traverse the entire length of the Milky Way. What's even more amazing is that once you're there, you've barely left the front yard!

Now consider this: This vast and complex universe is only temporary. One day, Peter tells us, "the heavens will pass away with a terrible noise, and everything in them will disappear in fire, and the earth and everything on it will be exposed to judgment" (2 Peter 3:10). The present universe, as glorious as it is, will give way to a new heaven and a new earth that will far exceed this one in glory. We'll be living in glorified resurrected bodies in a renewed earthly environment during the kingdom age and a completely new environment in the eternal state. We will never grow old, we will never suffer.

How Does Heaven Motivate You?

Do you care that some people are *not* going to be there with Jesus in his glory? Does the certainty of heaven so grip you that you are motivated to invite as many people there as you can? Can you honestly be content to go to heaven alone? Does the imminent return of Jesus Christ prompt you to look beyond your own little world to become involved in God's worldwide work of kingdom building?

Not long ago I went to a lockdown ward in a local hospital to speak with a girl who was suffering from depression and was suicidal. I spoke kindly to her, realizing she was probably traumatized from something in her life. But I also went out on a limb and spoke firmly. Sometimes such patients can be utterly self-focused and need to be encouraged to look beyond their own existence. There can be a horrible paralysis in self-analysis. An inward searching and probing can often be consuming. "You know, it's not all about you," I said. She looked back at me with astonishment. "God has work for you to do. His plan for you isn't over yet. There are other people who need you." I could tell she hadn't been thinking along those lines. The only spotlight shining in her little world was on her. My remarks prompted her to think differently. Two weeks later, this same girl approached me at church and thanked me for the gentle jolt back to reality. She was lifted out of her darkness when she discovered that her life had a greater purpose and that God was interested in using her. She was now determined to find out exactly what God's purpose was for her life.

❖ ❖ ❖

HOW ARE YOU PREPARING FOR HEAVEN NOW?

Jesus told us to "store [our] treasures in heaven" (Matthew 6:20); that is, to put our temporal resources to work for future purposes. Earthly treasure can be used for God's glory by investing it in heaven where it will last eternally. The way we spend our time and money indicates the condition of our heart and the level of our preparedness for heaven. Jesus asked, "How do you benefit if you gain the whole world but lose or forfeit your own soul in the process?" (Luke 9:25). Ask yourself, *Do I have a saved soul but a wasted life?*

Before the end of your life on earth, what will you have done to prepare for your eternal stay in heaven? Storing up treasures in heaven means to use all that we have for God's glory *now* so that we can enjoy God's glory to the fullest later. Heaven is guaranteed for every disciple, but our position in heaven is not. Paul reveals that "we must all stand before Christ to be judged. We will each receive whatever we deserve for the good or evil we have done in our bodies" (2 Corinthians 5:10). Once we're in heaven, Christ will evaluate our life on earth and he will reward us according to how we used what he entrusted to us to expand his kingdom. This doesn't refer to a judgment of our sins; that's been taken care of at the Cross. But we'll be evaluated based on all the activities we did during our lifetime on earth. What we as Christians do here and now in our temporal bodies will have an impact for all eternity: "There is going to come a time of testing at the judgment day to see what kind of work each builder has done. Everyone's work will be put through the fire to see whether or not it keeps its value. If the work survives the fire, that builder will receive a reward. But if the work is burned up, the builder will suffer great loss. The builders themselves will be saved, but like someone escaping through a wall of flames" (1 Corinthians 3:13-15).

You can prepare for heaven right now by using your time, talent, and treasure to help people come to know Christ, grow in Christ, and live for Christ. Are you doing that? If so, what a glorious future you're building! Yes, you can make it to heaven in the very final moments of your life, like the thief on the cross. My friend Tony did, and others have as well. But why do that? Why just barely get in? Why not get in with honors? Peter tells us to live in such a way that "an entrance will be supplied to you *abundantly* into the everlasting kingdom of our Lord and Savior Jesus Christ" (2 Peter 1:11, NKJV, emphasis added). It's best to have a saved soul and a useful life. Don't squander your present; invest it for the future.

A little boy and his father got into an elevator in the Empire State Building and began their upward journey. The boy watched the flashing numbers as the elevator rose past each of the floors: 10 . . . 20 . . . 30 . . . 40 . . . 50 . . . 60 . . . 70. As they kept going, the boy got nervous. Finally he grabbed his father's hand and blurted out, "Daddy, does God know we're coming?"

The truth is, God *does* know we're coming. And he knows exactly when we'll arrive. He's ready for us. The question is, are we ready for eternity? Are we ready to be forever with Christ? I don't mean, are we looking forward to getting off this sin-scarred earth and enjoying eternal bliss? But are we truly prepared? Have we invested wisely for the future?

When I was in Egypt several years ago, all I really wanted to see were the great pyramids at Giza. I got my wish. On a hot spring afternoon, I stood gazing at those wonders of the ancient world, the burial places of the pharaohs. Some have estimated that it required the efforts of one hundred thousand workers working full time for forty years to build one of the great pyramids. Why did the ancient Egyptians devote such intense labor to the project? Why so much effort? Why so much emphasis on the afterlife? Although they were misled theologically, they were right about one point: The Egyptians understood that they would spend a lot more time in the afterlife than they spent in this life.

14

PRAYING NOW WHILE LOOKING AHEAD

*H*ow does Jesus' prayer that we be united with him in future glory help us pray now? Remember, Jesus didn't pray this prayer silently while he was alone. He prayed in the presence of his disciples, and John recorded what he heard. Obviously, Jesus intended for his prayer to motivate his followers. And I believe his prayer for future glory can motivate our prayers today.

Jesus never intended for our focus on heaven to distract us from our responsibilities on earth. Rather, he saw that our future hope would make us *more* fit to live here and now. As John later wrote, "We can't even imagine what we will be like when Christ returns. But we do know that when he comes we will be like him, for we will see him as he really is. And all who believe this will keep themselves pure, just as Christ is pure" (1 John 3:2-3). Our anticipation of the future should motivate our purity in the present.

As I write these words, I am sitting in an airport waiting to catch a flight home. I've been pushing to get home a little sooner, but several flights have been canceled due to weather. Nevertheless, I'm willing to do what needs to be done in order to catch an outbound flight so I can be reunited with my family. The goal of the reunion is worth the inconvenience of a rearranged schedule, taxis to other terminals, or longer waits.

After Jesus' death and resurrection, the disciples were distracted from their daily responsibilities for a time. Before Jesus ascended, they asked about the future kingdom and whether or not Jesus would unveil it right there and then (Acts 1:6). Jesus brought their gaze back down to earth, telling them to represent him and spread the news of the kingdom to the far ends of the earth. And when Jesus ascended into heaven, as these same men stood with their heads pointed upward as if to anticipate the coming kingdom, angels reaffirmed their immediate and ongoing mission: "Men of Galilee, why are you standing here staring at the sky? Jesus has been taken away from you into heaven. And someday, just as you saw him go, he will return!" (Acts 1:11). That *someday* wasn't *that day*. Until the day when Christ returns in his glory, every disciple has a responsibility to live in the present while anticipating the future. Knowing that one day we who are inglorious shall be glorified, how should we pray?

⬧ ⬧ ⬧

PRAY FOR YOURSELF AS A DISCIPLE

Pray for the best use of your life on earth. The day will soon come when we will never again be able to witness to an unbeliever. Once we're in heaven, there will be no need to preach the gospel because unbelievers won't be there! We'll no longer have the opportunity to lead someone to Christ. Evangelism is strictly earthbound. Paul encourages us to live wisely: "So be careful how you live, not as fools but as those who are wise. Make the most of every opportunity for doing good in these evil days. Don't act thoughtlessly, but try to understand what the Lord wants you to do" (Ephesians 5:15-17).

As a chaplain for the FBI, I work with fine men and women who lay their lives on the line daily. For them, facing death is a part of life. When we're together, we talk freely about this. Recently, an agent friend of mine collapsed suddenly from a grand mal seizure. He had no medical history that would have indicated a preexisting condition or elevated risk. But the past is no guarantee of the future. After two brain scans, a sizable tumor was discovered in his right temporal lobe. Its size and location demanded surgery—and soon. This man, a strong Christian, now realizes even more that eternity may not be far away. He asked me to pray with him that he would use this experience and the time he has left to spread God's message of love to others. Knowing that he may soon be glorified has heightened his sense of urgency for the present.

That's how we all should live, because the truth is, we're all in the same boat as my friend. David was right; he spoke for all of us when he said to his friend Jonathan, "I am only a step away from death" (1 Samuel 20:3). It could happen to anyone at any moment. We see evidence of that every day. Pray for yourself to make the right decisions and take the right action in the time you have left—whether that time is marked in days or decades. Jesus said that we should be storing up for ourselves "treasures in heaven" (Matthew 6:20). We should be looking ahead to our life beyond the grave. Pray for wisdom in the use of your finances, time, and opportunities. Pray that every day will count for something eternal. At the end of one of his parables, Jesus admonished his followers to "use your worldly resources to benefit others and make friends. In this way, your generosity stores up a reward for you in heaven" (Luke 16:9). One day we will all stand before Christ's judgment seat; his kingdom *will have* come. What rewards will you receive there for your time spent here? Remember, it's possible to have a saved soul but a wasted life.

✤ ✤ ✤

PRAY FOR NON-DISCIPLES

Part of our role as Christ's disciples here on earth is to touch the lives of those who aren't yet his disciples. For unbelievers, the idea of eternity is ridiculous and nonessential. It may motivate us, but it merely distracts them. They don't see what we see. They don't think about what we think about. It can sometimes be frustrating to talk to these people—like trying to describe a colorful sunset to a blind man or a moving symphony to someone who is deaf. So what do we do? We pray for them. We talk to them about heaven and hell. We live exemplary lives for them to observe. And we continue to pray for them. That's why we're still "in the world"; we're here for the benefit of those who are not yet saved. We may be looking forward to God's kingdom in glory, but we're praying for God's kingdom to come here on earth right now in the lives of our friends, our neighbors, and our enemies. In a spiritual sense, wherever Jesus is, there his kingdom is also. When someone is born again, he or she enters the kingdom of God.

The future glory we anticipate should motivate us to pray for those who are not yet saved. "Since everything around us is going to melt away, what holy, godly lives you should be living! You should look forward to that day and *hurry it along*—the day when God will set the heavens on fire and the elements will melt away in the flames. But we are looking forward to the new heavens and new earth he has promised, a world where everyone is right with God" (2 Peter 3:11-13, emphasis added).

Isn't it interesting that we can actually hurry that day along? How can we do that? By living godly lives before unbelievers and praying that the kingdom will come to them too. We will never have a redemptive impact upon an unbelieving world without prayer. "I urge you, first of all, to pray for all people," wrote Paul to his young friend Timothy. "As you make your requests, plead for God's mercy upon them . . . for he wants everyone to be saved and to understand the truth" (1 Timothy 2:1, 4).

PRAY FOR DISTRACTED DISCIPLES

Distracted disciples are ones who have forgotten about eternity and are consumed by the immediate and the temporary. They are ones for whom the reality of future glory has lost its luster. To distracted disciples, heaven is such a distant place and not of much present value. Temporal things such as careers, business deals, stocks, homes—and even family and church—greatly overshadow any thoughts of future glory. Even though the amount of time we will spend on earth is minuscule compared to the endless span of eternity, it seems that every distracted disciple's eggs are all in one temporal basket.

Distracted disciples are all around us, and they need our prayer. And we must guard our own hearts as well, lest we become distracted from our heavenly purpose. We must pray in the same way the prophet Elisha prayed for his servant, "Lord, I pray, open his eyes that he may see" into the spiritual realm that is more real and powerful than the earthly realm (2 Kings 6:17, NKJV). Distracted disciples have a foreshortened perspective that renders them ineffective. Prayer can make all the difference. If God will open their eyes and elevate their perspective beyond the mundane and the ordinary, their lives—and their effectiveness—could be supercharged to a higher voltage.

Another form of distraction is found within the body of Christ. Infighting between Christian denominations, church factions, and divergent movements has long been a distraction that undermines our effectiveness. Isn't it odd that the very ones with whom we will be spending eternity are the very ones we're bickering with now? Some would say that in heaven we'll all be glorified, making getting along so much easier, but shouldn't we at least try to get along with each other now?

A janitor in a Scottish church found a crumpled note beneath the pews after a Sunday service. It expressed the sentiments of one disgruntled saint:

> To dwell above with those we love will certainly be glory;
>   But to dwell below with those we know; now that's a different story!

Why do we allow petty differences of style and form to distract us from our common mission to reach a lost world? We need to pray for distracted disciples whose infighting is making them an eyesore to non-disciples. Pray for reconciliation within the fractured body of Christ. I was once introduced to a fellow clergyman in our community whose first words to me were, "Well, I thought I'd come and check out the competition!" What an unfortunate perspective. Rather than "competing," we ought to be finding ways to cooperate—to complement and strengthen each other's ministries. I surely don't want our focus on our individual ministries to distract us from our mutual goal—to be together in the presence of the glorified Christ.

✚ ✚ ✚

PRAY FOR THRESHOLD DISCIPLES

Threshold disciples are those whose life on earth is nearing a close. The hope and promise of eternity is especially meaningful to the elderly and the terminally ill. They will likely see this prayer of Jesus answered sooner than the rest of us. Their impending physical death will carry them across the threshold and into the fullness of eternal life. Still, the loneliness that often accompanies these believers in their final days of life can be monumental. They need our prayers to keep them focused on what lies ahead. Toward the end of their life on earth, many look back in remorse as they recall their failures and foibles. Pray that these threshold disciples will be able to say as Paul did, "I am still not all I should be, but I am focusing all my energies on this one thing: Forgetting the past and looking forward to what lies ahead" (Philippians 3:13). Glory in the presence of our God and our Savior is what lies ahead for threshold believers; pray that their last moments on earth won't be consumed by the gloom of the past.

Pray for a sense of eagerness for these threshold disciples. Some, toward the end of their lives, feel fearful. It's as if an overwhelming spirit of doubt overtakes them in their final hours. They may question the security of their salvation even if they have faithfully walked with the Lord for years. Satan, who always looks for opportunities to attack us, will try to rob us of our peace during this time of passing. Pray that these dying believers may keep their eyes on the prize that awaits them. When Paul was writing his final words, his swan song, he said, "As for me, my life has already been poured out as an offering to God. The time of my death is near. I have fought a good fight, I have finished the race, and I have remained faithful. And now the prize awaits me—the crown of righteousness that the Lord, the righteous Judge, will give me on that great day of his return. And the prize is not just for me but for all who eagerly look forward to his glorious return" (2 Timothy 4:6-8). The glory of God is very near to threshold believers; pray that the thought of impending glory will be an encouragement and comfort to them.

◼ ◼ ◼

PRAY FOR PERSECUTED DISCIPLES

Christians around the world are suffering for their faith in Christ. The persecuted church is as much a reality today as it was in the first few centuries of the Common Era, when Christianity spread throughout the Roman Empire. It has been estimated that more martyrs were produced in the twentieth century than in all other centuries combined since the time of Christ. Here in the United States we may not be as aware of persecution, but we must intercede in prayer on behalf of our persecuted brothers and sisters in other nations. Most of the disciples who were with Jesus on the night when he prayed went on to die gruesome deaths. Other disciples were burned at the stake, stoned, or thrown to wild animals that tore their flesh in the coliseums of the Roman provinces. But with the persistence of repressive governments and the rise of virulent, radical Islam and other religious movements, Christians around the world are suffering in increasing numbers right now.

I've spoken to persecuted believers in jungles, deserts, and inner cities around the world. I've discovered that they need encouragement and prayer. Whenever I've asked them how Christians in the West can help, almost invariably their answer is, "Pray for us!" But how? What should we pray? Pray that, like the threshold disciples, they will focus on what is ahead of them and what is at stake around them. Pray that their witness may be firm and confident and pleasing to the Lord. Pray that the persecution will not be wasted but will be used to bring their persecutors to salvation. Pray that they may see themselves as Jesus sees them—part of an elite company of infantry for God's kingdom. "God blesses you when you are mocked and persecuted and lied about because you are my followers. Be happy about it! Be very glad! For a great reward awaits you in heaven. And remember, the ancient prophets were persecuted, too" (Matthew 5:11-12).

❖ ❖ ❖

PRAY FOR A FRESH PERSPECTIVE ON LIFE

What will your life on earth mean in eternity? One hundred years from now, it won't matter what kind of car you drove, what kind of house you built, what your bank accounts and investment portfolios looked like, or how chic your clothes were. It won't matter what school you graduated from, whether you had the latest and fastest computer, or how big your church was. What *will* matter one hundred years from now is how you spent your life preparing for eternity in heaven. C. S. Lewis was right when he wrote: "All that is not eternal is eternally out of date."[1]

15

SHOULD WE PRAY LIKE GOD PRAYS?

ℵow that we've examined the prayer of Jesus, a question still remains: Should we pray like God prays? After all, didn't Jesus give his disciples another example to use as a template for their prayers? (See Luke 11:1-4; Matthew 6:9-13.) In fact, in Matthew 6:9 Jesus plainly tells the disciples, "Pray like this." On the other hand, let's not forget that Jesus prayed audibly in John 17 so that his disciples could hear him. Could it be, then, that Jesus was modeling the same prayer he had earlier taught his disciples to pray? Let's take a look.

❖ ❖ ❖

OUR FATHER IN HEAVEN . . .

When Jesus taught the disciples to address God as their "Father in heaven" (Matthew 6:9), he was telling them that they could have their own relationship with God like a child would enjoy with his father. They had the right to enter his presence. Furthermore, he is approachable. There was no distance to be breached before they could come, no ritual to engage in, and no hoops to jump through. So long as they were disciples of Jesus Christ, they could enjoy access to the Father. Using the term *Father* implies familiarity and relational intimacy. And that's exactly how Jesus himself spoke when he prayed. He "looked up to heaven and said, 'Father . . .'" (John 17: 1; also verses 5, 11, 21, 24, and 25). Jesus prayed the same way he had taught his men to pray. This familial and familiar approach could be enjoyed because the disciples had become children of God by faith—and so have we! The apostle Paul writes, "Because you are sons, God sent the Spirit of his Son into our hearts, the Spirit who calls out, 'Abba, Father'" (Galatians 4:6, NIV). The word *Abba* is both the Aramaic and the Hebrew term for "Daddy" or "Papa." Today in Israel one can hear the high-pitched refrains of young children calling after their fathers: "Abba! Abba! Abba!" Jesus himself used the name *Abba* when addressing his Father in heaven (Mark 14:36).

But in what way is God *our* Father, since we aren't part of the Godhead? Someone might argue that, in a generically spiritual way, all human beings are children of God. In one sense they'd be correct, but in another, more important sense, they'd be very wrong. Every person is a child of God *by creation,* but only certain ones have become children of God *by redemption.* In the beginning, God created humanity in his own image (Genesis 1:27). Consequently, everyone bears the image of God to some degree, even though we have fallen away from God's original intent. However, Jesus said, "To all who believed him [meaning himself, the Messiah] and accepted him, he gave the right to become children of God" (John 1:12). Whenever a person comes to God through faith in the finished work of Jesus Christ on the cross, a new level of relationship opens up. This is what Jesus meant when he referred to being "born again"(John 3:1-8). Only a spiritual birth enables spiritual life and a spiritual relationship with God in heaven. When we are born again by the Spirit, God is no longer just our God but he also becomes our Father in heaven.

❖ ❖ ❖

HALLOWED BE YOUR NAME . . .

After addressing God as Father, Jesus told his disciples to revere the name of God. The archaic English word *hallow,* carried forward from the King James Version of the Bible, means to honor, respect, or venerate. This implies much more than a formalized acknowledgment of God's sovereign position. In ancient times, one's name was tantamount to one's character. Thus to honor God's name is to glorify God himself. That, according to Jesus, is to be the main thrust of our prayer lives—and our lives in general. A good and wise habit to develop is to filter every request in prayer through one simple question: If God were to answer this prayer, would it bring glory to his reputation?

When Jesus prays in John 17, he follows the same pattern of glorifying God: "Father, the time has come. Glorify your Son *so he can give glory back to you*" (John 17:1, emphasis added). Jesus could request glory because he is himself God, but the aim of his prayer was to bring the Father honor—to "hallow" his name. He also summed up his life on earth according to the same goal when he prayed, "I brought glory to you here on earth" (John 17:4).

❖ ❖ ❖

YOUR KINGDOM COME . . .

Knowing that our prayers can easily tilt in a selfish direction, Jesus taught his disciples to pray with certain priorities in mind. Rather than jumping right in with our requests or telling God about our needs, we must maintain a balance of priorities. Jesus instructed the disciples to pray, "May your Kingdom come soon. May your will be done here on earth, just as it is in heaven" (Matthew 6:10). God is concerned about *everything* in our lives, but the purpose of prayer is not to further our own kingdoms or to insist on our own will being done. Rather it is to see God's will accomplished on earth. The purpose of prayer, in part, is to align our will with God's agenda, to see where he is moving, and to discern how to align ourselves with his purpose.

This is exactly the sense of priority that Jesus displays when he prays, "I brought glory to you here on earth *by doing everything you told me to do*" (John 17:4, emphasis added). His entire life on earth was devoted to furthering the Father's agenda. To the anxious crowds who wanted to crown him, Jesus replied, "I have come down from heaven to do the will

❖ ❖ ❖

LEAD US NOT INTO
TEMPTATION . . .

The disciples faced a difficult road. Soon Satan would focus his attack against them. For this reason, Jesus taught the disciples to pray, "Don't let us yield to temptation, but deliver us from the evil one" (Matthew 6:13). The evil one and his minions would push hard against Jesus' loyal adherents by using a vast armory of ploys designed to tempt their flesh. Leaning hard on God's help in prayer would become an essential part of their survival.

Throughout his ministry on earth, Jesus had already battled the devil successfully. He was aware of Satan's style and intensity. Early on, Jesus was tempted by the devil (Matthew 4:1-11). Satan continued to look for opportunities to attack Jesus throughout his life's work (Luke 4:13), and he worked hard at orchestrating Jesus' betrayal by a close associate at the end of his ministry (John 13:2). Even though Jesus himself didn't pray to be kept from temptation, he prayed that his followers would be protected. "I'm not asking you to take them out of the world, but to keep them safe from the evil one" (John 17:15). Knowing that spiritual warfare is a constant reality, he preempted Satan's barrage on the disciples.

It's amazing to realize that Jesus Christ, the unique Son of God, not only prayed for his immediate disciples, but he also prayed for you and me two thousand years ago. As he faced his own "ground zero," his imminent torture and death by crucifixion, he thought of you and me. Even more amazing is the realization that he continues to pray for us today in his role as High Priest. He prays that we will be kept secure from Satan's blasting attacks. He prays that we will be strengthened in our testimony and firm in our unity as we are on our way to heaven. He provided the way for us to get there and he wants to make sure we arrive safely.

Steve Winger of Lubbock, Texas, tells a delightful story about a final exam in a logic class known for its difficulty. The professor had told his classroom full of nervous students that they could bring as much information to the test as they could fit on a single piece of notebook paper. Most of the students crammed as many facts as possible on their $8\frac{1}{2}$-by-11 sheet of paper. They etched answers and concepts in tiny script across both sides, hoping to include all the information they would need to pass the test. One student, however, interpreted the professor's directive a bit differently. On the day of the test, he walked into class, placed a sheet of notebook paper on the floor in front of his desk, then had an advanced student of logic stand on the paper. After all, the professor had said he could bring as much information as he could fit on a single piece of paper. The advanced student was able to whisper the correct answers, and the resourceful student was the only one to get an A on the test![1]

We are in a similar position with Jesus Christ. Not only is he available to provide the answers we need for our lives, he *is* the answer for our lives. He already stood in for us at the final exam. Not only did he take the judgment for our sins upon himself, he continues to intercede on our behalf—even now—before the Father. With Christ as our advocate, the victory will surely be ours!

16

ANTIDOTE TO A BORING PRAYER LIFE

A survey reported in *U.S. News and World Report* said that 41 percent of Americans are bored at work; 48 percent are bored by what goes on in Washington; and 70 percent of junior high and high school students are bored at school.[1] I wonder how many people are bored with what's going on in heaven or what God is doing on earth? Let's face it: for many, prayer is just plain boring! At times it can seem like you're just speaking into the air. Talking to God is different than talking to people, after all, because when you speak with friends, you can *see* them and observe their responses.

Although God is invisible and transcendent, we can still have a relationship with him that is satisfying and enjoyable. Prayer is intended to be an expression of *relationship* rather than a *ritual* or even a *responsibility*. It can be and should be a delight. At the same time, every relationship involves a measure of responsibility. I can't have a meaningful relationship without being responsible to nurture that relationship to some degree. If I truly treasure my relationships, however, the responsibility involved won't become a burden. I will view my opportunities for interaction and fellowship as a blessing, a way to connect with the other person in a meaningful way. That's how prayer should be in our relationship with God.

My home is perched cozily in a green, five-acre cove of pine trees nestled in the lower Rockies at an altitude of 7,800 feet. The drive from town isn't terribly long and I thrive on the sense of "going up" to such an inviting isolation. Looking eastward out my study window, thirty feet above the rocky ground below, I get a feeling of being suspended between heaven and earth. The light dances in the mountains of New Mexico in a way I've not seen anywhere else, making early mornings and late afternoons nearly magical experiences. These golden hours are times I treasure. They are unquestionably the best part of the day for me—and they are times I love to talk to the Maker of these places and times. Prayer comes alive for me in these mountains—and I never pray with my eyes closed here!

But I don't want to mislead you. Prayer doesn't require a certain altitude, nor does it demand pristine surroundings for it to thrive. Jesus' greatest prayer, as we've seen in this book, was in the city where he would soon be murdered on a Roman cross. Paul's prayers were uttered from jail cells, a pain-filled sickbed, an isolated desert, and a prison ship. There's never a lag time in prayer between earth and heaven, whether you're in a crowded city subway, a fetid and noisy third-world bus, or a quiet mountain glen. But there is an inviting isolation with prayer. The alluring appeal of separating yourself unto God is what makes prayer so delightful. Getting alone and "going up" with God into transcendent union with him—it really doesn't get any better than this!

Why do so many people regard prayer as a struggle or an annoyance? Why is it confined to the dinner table and church services? Why, whenever it is addressed from the pulpit, do people get that look on their faces—like they've mistakenly stepped into the wrong building on the wrong weekend; or like a waiter messed up their order and brought a peanut-butter sandwich instead of filet mignon?

A man in my congregation approached me recently, his face chiseled with sincerity. "Pastor," he said, "why can't we get more people to pray? I just can't understand it. There should be more who are interested in this stuff!" This fellow leads a prayer ministry that meets during our church services to pray for those who have gathered. Everyone who participates in these times of prayer reports a thrilling experience. They tell me they can't stay away. But only a handful come each Sunday. Why so few? Why not more? Why does it take a war or a national catastrophe to motivate people to take spiritual matters seriously?

❖ ❖ ❖

PRAYER SESSION OR YAWN SESSION?

There must be as many answers to the above questions as there are people, but here are a couple of my own observations. First, we humans are basically arrogant and spuriously self-sufficient creatures. We cherish independence and we loathe dependence. We love to replace prayer with programs—humanly inspired activities that can be "implemented" and that often require no reliance on God in order to work. Further, we replace our fellowship with God with church-related functions that we can plan and control. With prayer, we must be dependent; with programs, we can exercise our independence and individuality. To reduce such a lofty thing as prayer to redundant rituals and formulas seems to be a human tendency. It has always been that way.

My second observation is that because we tend to reduce prayer to a predictable pattern, we drain it of its spontaneity and freshness and it becomes boring. We've bottled it and packaged it like some kind of generic product for Christians. Chuck Swindoll admitted to his own struggles with this kind of prayer:

> If you had asked me twenty years or more ago
> if prayer was one of the essentials in an aimless
> world like ours, I would have surely said, "No."
> At least, not the brand of prayer I had been
> exposed to. It wasn't that I was unaware of the
> high profile prayer plays in the Bible. I was
> simply turned off by the exposure I had had.
> So I pretty well tuned it out.[2]

Sadly, a lot of other people have had a similar experience with prayer and have "tuned it out." But maybe it's our own fault. Perhaps we're the ones who have decided to relegate prayer to the category of boring activities. Subconsciously, we know that prayer is important, but we see it as a chore, a duty, a contractual obligation of being a Christian. "Now that I'm a Christian, I guess that this is something I just *gotta* do!" It reminds me of a story I heard about two girls who were sitting together in church. They sat through the hymns, the homilies, and the prayers, and finally in disgust the younger one sighed out loud, "This is boring!" Her sister, jumping at the opportunity to act more mature and grown up, nudged her and whispered, "Shhh! It's supposed to be boring—it's church!" Who taught that little girl to think like that? And who taught us? We may not be as forthcoming as the two sisters, but we tacitly agree.

Why is it that we take something as simple as talking to God and complicate it, making it dreary and uninteresting? Where is it written that prayer has to be boring? Someone suggested that if theologians were to rewrite what Jesus instructed his disciples to pray, "Give us this day our daily bread," it might sound more like this:

> We respectfully petition, request & entreat that due & adequate provision be made, this day and the date hereinafter subscribed, for the satisfying of these petitioners' nutritional requirements and for the organizing of such methods of allocation and distribution as many as may be deemed necessary and proper to assure the reception by and for said petitioners of such

> quantities of baked cereal products as shall,
> in the judgment of the aforesaid petitioners,
> constitute a sufficient supply thereof.

Could it be that we've inadvertently made prayer into something that God never intended? We've made it hard, painful, rigid, and even agonizing. And then we walk away from it all, feeling guilty that it wasn't enough! We didn't pray hard enough; it wasn't long enough or sincere enough; we didn't use the right words; we didn't stay focused; we didn't vociferate loudly enough; we didn't believe as intensely as we should have. Is that what God intends for us to feel after a session of prayer? Should we automatically give ourselves an F in this spiritual curriculum? It doesn't sound quite right, does it? You'll be relieved to know that such a response isn't biblical either!

Prayer was never meant to be a yawn session packed with enough boredom to cure your aunt's insomnia. Neither does God want us to walk away from our talks with him burdened with megadoses of anxiety and guilt. The exact opposite should occur. Prayer was designed to convert anxiety into tranquility! It should produce a sense of peace. Listen to Paul's words:

> Don't worry about anything; instead, pray about everything. Tell God what you need, and thank him for all he has done. If you do this, you will experience God's peace, which is far more wonderful than the human mind can understand.

His peace will guard your hearts and minds as you live in Christ Jesus. (Philippians 4:6-7)

Did you catch that? Prayer should cultivate peace, not panic; it should produce an inward serenity rather than shame. We can see traces of this in Jesus' prayer. He doesn't recite a bunch of dusty, traditional mumbo jumbo; nor does he give off a sense of alarm or anxiety. Jesus' prayer is filled with confidence, anticipation, and peace, even though he is facing his own imminent execution. Why should our experience with prayer be any less peaceful, confident, and optimistic?

❖ ❖ ❖

POURING A NEW FOUNDATION

The best part about the cozy setting of my mountain home is the part that no one sees—the foundation. It's as solid as the mountain itself. In fact, it *is* the mountain itself! When the builders cleared the lot, they discovered that the rock shelf that underlies the building site is deeper than any concrete slab could ever be. I now rest at night knowing that the footings of our home are drilled directly into existing bedrock. How different from so many of the seaside homes I grew up around in southern California. Those picturesque homes overlooking the Pacific are undergirded by steel pilings and concrete, but sometimes the forces of nature are too strong and send the houses out for an unexpected swim. The foundation is everything!

Let me suggest a brand new foundation for your prayer life. It's time to dig down deeper. It's time to sink your footings into the bedrock of God.

Have you ever heard new Christians pray? They may not be very refined. They may not use all the familiar, spiritual-sounding words and phrases that we use. But when they pray, it's *fresh*. They sound like they're really talking to someone! Once, while visiting the eastern seaboard for a men's retreat, I had an opportunity to pray with a recently converted New York City steelworker. This guy was a welder who had grown up around the rough Manhattan labor crews. When he prayed, it was like stepping into a gangster movie, only it was genuine with this guy. He began, "Yo! Lord, listen! I don't know what ta say to ya, but I really need ya help, ya know watta mean?" At first I chuckled to myself, but I was quickly impressed by how *real* his prayer was. No one had told him yet to say *thee, thou,* and *thine,* and *if it be thy will.* He just laid it out there for the Lord to hear. I can assure you that our prayer time together was anything but boring!

King David, Israel's sweet psalmist, recorded more than one hundred examples of prayer that have inspired generations. I love one of his descriptions of the process: "O my people, trust in him at all times. *Pour out your heart to him,* for God is our refuge" (Psalm 62:8, emphasis added). Have you ever thought of prayer like that before? As *pouring out* the contents of your heart to God? Nothing is left; everything is brought forth. This isn't the picture of an austere and boring exercise. David encourages us to let it all hang out before God in prayer. Like pouring out a pitcher of old, sour milk, you can unload your heart before God. Like pouring out a vial of the finest perfume, you can lavish your praise on him. Rather than presenting your neatly packaged protocol prayers, allow your heart to flow.

A FOUNDATION FOR POWERFUL PRAYER

𝒥n this final chapter, I want to help you establish a new foundation for prayer by taking the principles we've considered and setting them as cornerstones upon which you can build your daily prayer time. It is my hope that these principles modeled by Jesus will transform your communication with God.

❖ ❖ ❖

CORNERSTONE #1:
MAKE GOD YOUR GOAL,
NOT YOUR GATEWAY.

Tell God how much you appreciate his care, concern, and control. Tell him you want to magnify him and do whatever he wants.

✤ Learn to make God's glory your sole purpose. Filter every request through this question: "If God answers my prayer, how will it magnify *his* reputation?" Is pleasing God the purpose of your request, or are your motives selfish?

✛ Refuse to complain to God about his gifts to you or of his treatment of you. It only insults God when we grumble about our lot in life, and it robs us of the joy that prayer can bring.

✛ Follow Jesus' example and determine to obey God, no matter what. Make it your goal to be able to say honestly, as Jesus said, "I have glorified You on the earth" (John 17:4, NKJV).

▨ ▨ ▨

CORNERSTONE #2: ENJOY GOD.

Practice just "being" with God. Bask in his presence. Tell him what he means to you. Sing a song to him occasionally to keep your prayer fresh. Confess your sins to him so that your access will be unrestricted.

✛ Don't be quick to request—or demand—things from God. Take time to enjoy him. Remember, Jesus did not immediately request things for his disciples. First he spoke to God about his relationship with his disciples and their relationship with the Father. This is a good model. Prayer should be a deepening of our relationship with God, not an opportunity to present our demands.

✣ Prayer is a means of association *with* God. It isn't a means of passing on information *to* God. You are not dropping off a wish list. Prayer should be a delight, not a duty.

▩ ▧ ▩

CORNERSTONE #3:
PRAY FOR PERMEATION NOT SEGREGATION.

Ask God to keep you holy amid an unholy world. Ask for courage to face the challenge of permeating the culture with God's unique truth. Ask God to use his Word to equip you for service. Ask him daily for specific truths to practice and apply.

✣ True holiness is accomplished through the Scriptures. Bible study and prayer go hand in hand.

✣ Refuse to pray escapist prayers even though the world system may seem ominous to you.

✣ Recognize that spiritual warfare is going on around you. Satan wants to undermine your desire for holiness so that you'll have no viable message to share with and challenge the world.

✣ Refuse to isolate yourself from the world. Pray that God would open up opportunities for you to be in the world (but not of it) as a shining example of how Jesus Christ can change a person's life. Avoid isolationist excuses such as "I'm not called to evangelize"; "I'm not gifted in that area" (how *has* God gifted you?); "I don't have time."

✣ ✣ ✣

CORNERSTONE #4:
DON'T TRY TO GO IT ALONE.

Pray for the other Christian churches in your community. Repent of any divisiveness. Ask for discernment to differentiate between things that are essential and things that aren't. Ask God to use you to heal wounds between church groups.

- ✣ Don't forsake the fellowship of other believers. Pray together and "think of ways to encourage one another to outbursts of love and good deeds" (Hebrews 10:24).
- ✣ You're not the only true Christian left. He has many others who are part of his family.
- ✣ Creating a sense of family begins with your prayers and should be seen by your peers.
- ✣ Unity and love between Christians is what will convince the world that Jesus is worth considering.
- ✣ Remember: Unity doesn't mean agreeing on everything or compromising essentials.

✣ ✣ ✣

CORNERSTONE #5:
LIVE RESPONSIBLY; THINK ETERNALLY.

Think about heaven, your final destination, and thank God that his plan of salvation includes you. Ask him to help you keep from being distracted by frivolous temporal concerns. Ask for wisdom to spend your time, finances, and talent so that nothing in your life is wasted but is invested for eternity.

✛ We're heaven-bound pilgrims, sent by God to have an impact on the world, not fall in love with it.

✛ Thinking daily about your eternal future will help you deal with present hardships and tasks.

✛ Remember to live today so as to "store your treasures in heaven" (Matthew 6:20).

❖ ❖ ❖

MEETING WITH GOD

The principles that Jesus modeled and taught deserve more than a superficial glance. These key elements can transform your meeting time with God and bring you into a more intimate and satisfying relationship with him. To help you commit these principles of prayer more easily to memory, let me suggest the acronym M-E-E-T-S, which is what a believer does with God when he or she prays.

Magnify God: Living to glorify God is the first priority of prayer. God's glory is our goal.

Enjoyment: Being in God's presence and enjoying his fellowship is vital. Praise and adore him.

Engage in Evangelism: Ask God to make you holy in an unholy world as you permeate it.

Teamwork: Unity in the church family is essential to our earthly witness. Ask for more of it.

Sighting Eternity: Ask God for an undistracted life as you march toward the glories of heaven.

Make prayer your new priority. As you put these principles into practice, they will become a part of your daily life—and the results will be lifelong and life changing.

Let me make you a promise. If you start using these elements in your prayer life, you'll begin to notice a change. You will experience a fresh new delight in talking to God. You'll also find yourself becoming more balanced when it comes to your relationships with other Christians. I'm convinced you'll discover a new richness and depth of joy in prayer, even if you've been praying for years. Incorporate the M-E-E-T-S prayer pattern into your daily get-together with God until it becomes second nature to you.

These elements of prayer will begin to shape your decisions, thoughts, and actions until they reflect the same priorities that Jesus lived for and prayed for. You will find that talking to God is thrilling rather than boring. Moreover, you'll begin to notice a new lightness in your soul as you learn to pour out your heart before God.

Outside the RCA building on Fifth Avenue in New York City, there is a giant statue of Atlas with his muscles bulging as he strains to hold the world on his shoulders. He epitomizes how so many people live their lives. They sweat and strain to balance the enormous weight of life's problems all alone.

Not far away, just across town, is Saint Patrick's Cathedral. Out front there is also a statue, but it's a bit different. The figure is that of Christ, who stands resolutely holding the world in one hand.

Which way would you rather live? Do you want the world on your shoulders, crushing and overwhelming you? Or would you rather let Jesus hold your world in his firm and capable hand? That's what prayer does—it places the load on the right set of shoulders. It gives Christ the burden—which he is more than capable of handling—and lets you live in peace. An old, familiar hymn sums it up well:

> Oh, what peace we often forfeit!
> Oh, what needless pain we bear,
> All because we do not carry
> Everything to God in prayer!

NOTES

INTRODUCTION
1. Edythe Draper, *Draper's Book of Quotations for the Christian World* (Wheaton, Ill.: Tyndale House, 1992), 104, #1848.

CHAPTER 2
1. Lilly Walters, *Secrets of Successful Speakers* (New York: McGraw-Hill, 1993), 19.
2. James Patterson and Peter Kim, *The Day America Told the Truth* (New York: Prentice Hall, 1991), 52.
3. Barna Research Online, *Goals and Priorities;* <www.barna.org/cgi-bin/PageCategory.asp?CategoryID=23>.
4. James Montgomery Boice, *The Gospel of John,* vol. 4 (Grand Rapids, Mich.: Zondervan, 1978), 337–38.
5. Juan Carlos Ortiz, *Disciple* (Carol Stream, Ill.: Creation House, 1975), 34–35.

CHAPTER 3
1. Edythe Draper, *Draper's Book of Quotations for the Christian World* (Wheaton, Ill.: Tyndale House, 1992), 552, #10019.
2. Ibid., #10016
3. Howard Hendricks, *Leadership* 5, no. 2.
4. Pat Robertson, *Answers to 200 of Life's Most Probing Questions* (Nashville: Thomas Nelson, 1984), 96.
5. Charles Spurgeon, *Spurgeon at His Best,* comp. by Tim Carter (Grand Rapids, Mich.: Baker, 1988), 63.

CHAPTER 5

1. *Today in the Word* (April 1989): 28.
2. Robert Boyd Munger, *My Heart—Christ's Home,* rev. ed. (Downer's Grove, Ill.: InterVarsity, 1986), 13–16.
3. Marilyn Fais, "Heart to Heart," *Today's Christian Woman,* from The Bible Illustrator 3.0, index # 2839.

CHAPTER 6

1. John White, *The Fight* (Downers Grove, Ill.: InterVarsity, 1976), 179.
2. Ibid., 180.

CHAPTER 7

1. Jerry Vines, *Exploring 1, 2, 3 John* (Neptune, N.J.: Loizeau Brothers, 1990), 73–74.
2. Paul Lee Tan, *Encyclopedia of 7,700 Illustrations* (Rockville, Md.: Assurance), 168–169.
3. John White, *The Fight* (Downers Grove, Ill.: InterVarsity, 1976), 78.
4. Eugene Peterson, *The Message* (Colorado Springs, Colo.: NavPress, 1993), 226.
5. Edythe Draper, *Draper's Book of Quotations for the Christian World* (Wheaton, Ill.: Tyndale House, 1992), 38, #692.
6. Tan, *Encyclopedia,* 471.

CHAPTER 8

1. Billy Graham, *The Billy Graham Christian Worker's Handbook* (Minneapolis, Minn.: World Wide Publications, 1996), 300–301.

CHAPTER 9

1. Joanne O'Brien and Martin Palmer, *The State of Religion Atlas* (New York: Simon and Schuster, 1993).
2. David Watson, *I Believe in the Church* (Grand Rapids, Mich.: Eerdmans, 1978), 352.
3. Billy Graham Center Archives; <www.wheaton.edu/bgc/archives/faq/13.htm>.

CHAPTER 10

1. Chuck Smith, pastor of Calvary Bible Chapel, Costa Mesa, California, conversation with the author.

CHAPTER 11

1. David Watson, *I Believe in the Church* (Grand Rapids, Mich.: Eerdmans, 1978), 347.

2. Adapted from James S. Hewett, *Illustrations Unlimited* (Wheaton, Ill.: Tyndale House, 1988), 125–126.

CHAPTER 12

1. Charles Spurgeon, *Spurgeon at His Best,* comp. by Tim Carter (Grand Rapids, Mich.: Baker, 1988), 305.
2. Warren Wiersbe, *Listen! Jesus is Praying* (Wheaton, Ill.: Tyndale House, 1986), 119.
3. John MacArthur Jr., *Jesus' Pattern of Prayer* (Chicago: Moody, 1981), 61.

CHAPTER 13

1. Edythe Draper, *Draper's Book of Quotations for the Christian World* (Wheaton, Ill.: Tyndale House, 1992), 308, #5680.

CHAPTER 14

1. C. S. Lewis, *The Four Loves* (New York: Harcourt Brace Jovanovich, 1960), 188.

CHAPTER 15

1. Steve Winger, *Leadership* 15, no. 4.

CHAPTER 16

1. *U.S. News and World Report*, June 24, 1991, 14.
2. Charles Swindoll, *Strengthening Your Grip* (Waco, Tex.: Word, 1982), 147.